Luke hadn't meant to love Holly.

She's too young, he thought, *too innocent. Holly, with her kind gentle ways and unpretentious attitude toward life; Holly, a woodland nymph who loves the forest and animals as much as I do; Holly, who doesn't know how beautiful she is or how her loveliness stirs my heart.*

He didn't know whether the music that he heard was made by the pines or was in his mind.

"Holly," he said softly, turning over on his side and propping up on his elbow, "do you hear that music?"

"Yes, Luke," a silver ribbon of laughter threaded through her voice. Her eyes were closed and her hair, dried to golden tendrils, curled against the darkness of the rock. She opened her eyes and almost wished she hadn't, for the vivid blue of Luke's eyes was so close to hers.

"It's the singing of the pines and the murmur of the creek mixed with the…cadence of your heart," she whispered to the tempo of the music. "Not everyone can hear it, Luke. It's the song of Tannehill." She couldn't look away from the blue of his eyes.

Dear Reader,

The book you are about to read is a special kind of romance written with you in mind. It combines the thrill of newfound romance and the inspiration of a shared faith. By combining the two, we offer you an alternative to promiscuity and superficial relationships. Now you can read a romantic novel—with the romance left intact.

Inspirational Romances from Thomas Nelson will introduce you to exciting places and to men and women very much involved in today's fast-paced world, yet searching for romance and love with commitment—for someone to cherish and be cherished by. You will enjoy sharing their experiences. Most of all you will be uplifted by a romance that involves much more than physical attraction.

Welcome to a special kind of book with a special kind of love.

Etta Wilson

Etta Wilson, Editor

Song Of Tannehill

Shirley Sanders

Romances

Thomas Nelson Publishers • Nashville • Camden • New York

Grateful acknowledgment is made
to Mrs. Margaret S. Douglass,
Chairman, Tannehill Furnace
and Foundry Commission, 1978-1979,

and to Mr. James R. Bennett,
state senator of Alabama, and
Chairman, Executive Committee,
Tannehill Furnace & Foundry Commission.

Published in Nashville, Tennessee, by Thomas Nelson, Inc. and
distributed in Canada by Lawson Falle, Ltd., Cambridge, Ontario.

Printed in the United States of America.

All of the characters in this book are fictitious. Any resemblance
to actual persons, living or dead, is purely coincidental.

Scripture quotations in this book are from the King James Version
of the Bible.

The chorus of the hymn "Sunrise" on page 189 is copyrighted
1924 by Hall-Mack Co. (c) Renewed 1952, the Rodeheaver Co.
Used by permission.

ISBN 0-8407-7356-0

To

My Mother and Father

Vassie and Curtis Sanders

The original Tannehill story began in 1830 with a small forge on the banks of Roupe's Creek in Tuscaloosa County, Alabama. The furnace produced molten charge for agricultural tools and bar iron beside the gentle stream that slowly wound its way through Roupe's Valley. Tannehill Ironworks was one of the largest producers of iron for the Confederacy. During the Civil War Wilson's Raiders destroyed the furnaces, the cast houses, the tramway, the saw mill, the grist mill, and the slave quarters.

For many years the old Tannehill furnaces lay in ruins, dark crumbled monuments to the beginning of Birmingham's iron and steel industry. Then, after a century, Furnace No. 1 was recharged in a festive historic event. Speeches by visiting dignitaries, cannon blasts, music by a military band, and a flag-raising ceremony added to the fevered excitement of the re-firing of the furnace. It is at this event that the story of *Song of Tannehill* begins.

Today the furnaces stand in majestic silence, flanked by evergreen forests and smoky folds of mountains. The site is listed in the National Register of Historic Places and is designated by the state of Alabama as the Tannehill Historical State Park. It is located off I-65, twelve miles below Bessemer on the way to Tuscaloosa, and covers 1,000 acres in Jefferson, Bibb, and Tuscaloosa Counties.

Chapter One

"There's just nothing we can do about it, Buddy," Holly Scott muttered, affectionately stroking the head of the big dog at her side, "nothing at all."

Holly sat on the edge of the porch and dejectedly rested her chin on her right knee, her other slim brown leg swinging deliberately out of time to the beat of the music in the distance. Her slender figure was hugged by faded jeans, rolled up so she could feel the slight breeze which occasionally stirred through the stately soaring pines.

Buddy groaned a response and burrowed his head between his front paws as if the whole thing were too much for him. He lifted mournful eyes to Holly, then closed them again as if by that action he could make everything go away.

"A festive historic event..." that's how the paper will read, she thought, *and it won't say a word about all the trash people littered on the park grounds, or how they scared the ducks and kittens or how they filled up the valley with gasoline fumes.*

She wound her slender arms about her knee and stared out at the sea of cars and campers which packed Tannehill Park. Every inch of parking space was filled.

9

Well, at least by staying here, I don't have to stand in that crowd in the sun to wait for some old pompous dignitary, Holly complained inwardly. *If he had any manners at all, he'd have been on time.*

John Scott, Tannehill Park Superintendent, had waited for the representative of the United States Department of the Interior until Holly had persuaded him to go on to the ceremony. She didn't want her father to miss an event he had planned and looked forward to just because the guest of honor was late. Holly visualized the missing man as she mused aloud.

"Let's see…old, fat from sitting at a desk in a soft government job, bald, flourishing a white handkerchief and mopping his brow from this heat…."

Holly sighed as the fall breeze floated over the ocean of vehicles and blew a strand of her hair across her face. She impatiently pushed the offending blonde lock back and resumed her waiting position.

They made quite a picture there on the porch of the old log cabin—Holly and her dog. There was something touching in the scene. She was a slender young woman whose hair was the color of corn silk ripened in a summer's sun and whose lips needed no artificial color to proclaim her womanhood. Swinging her bare legs and feet above the Alabama red clay, with her dog sleeping at her side, she was the centerpiece of a striking tableau.

The charm and essence of another time and place were heightened by the background of the log cabin with its roughhewn posts, old plank porch, and faded cedar shake roof.

And that's the way Luke Westford saw her as he rounded the bend and swung down into Roupe's Valley that hot September Sunday afternoon.

The big blue Catalina station wagon and white camper trailer moved slowly through the small lane between four rows of closely parked vehicles. Luke Westford stopped the car and spoke briefly to a Boy Scout directing traffic, then continued down the big circle drive and turned into the one remaining spot in the entire park, a slot left beside the first cabin.

"That spot's reserved," Holly called. Her words contained a tone that combined authority with extreme irritation.

There was no indication the man even heard Holly. He lowered the windows of the station wagon by pushbutton and swung his powerful frame out of the car. An Irish setter, which had been asleep in the back of the station wagon, jumped into the front seat. The man spoke briefly to the dog, pocketed his keys, and turned towards Holly.

"That spot is reserved," she said again, this time with a controlled, cool quality to her usually soft southern voice. Buddy sat up, his ears lifting at the unusual inflection in Holly's voice.

"I know. The Scout told me," the man said. "I'm—"

"Then why did you park there? It just so happens that place is reserved for the guest of honor." She tilted her chin. Her vexation was apparent.

The man, who had seemed at first to be in a hurry, appraised her slowly and intently from his tall rangy vantage. His sweeping glance surveyed the bare toes, the slim bare legs, her youthful slim figure, and up to her corn-silk tresses. The course of his inspection made a little row of goose bumps travel up Holly's spine to the base of her neck.

"Has the ceremony started?" the man asked casually, deliberately ignoring her admonition about the parking place.

"Obviously," she snapped, referring to the strains of

11

the "Battle Hymn of the Republic" which could be heard in the distance. "If you'll just listen."

Holly was amazed at the tone of her own voice. It wasn't like her to become so ruffled over something as trivial as a parking place.

"What's obvious," he countered urbanely, "is that you could use some lessons from Emily Post, my young lady."

"If you had any manners..., Sir," Holly used her most pronounced southern drawl, "you'd move your car. And, I'm not your young lady."

"You're right. You're not a young lady." He inflected a mock drawl into his own voice that put hers to shame. "My apologies Miss—Miss Scarlett."

He inclined his head, bowed slightly from the waist, and turning abruptly on his heel, walked briskly down the narrow dusty road in the direction of the music.

Holly stifled the impulse to hurl a final retort at his back and glared angrily at the man's strong powerful figure until he crossed the bridge leading to the furnace and disappeared around the bend. His faultlessly tailored navy suit and white shirt was lost to view behind the trees that overlaid the trail.

"Ready. Fire!" came the distant shout.

Cannon blasts filled the air, and Buddy shifted to his feet and growled. The Irish setter in the station wagon bounded from the front seat into the back, and Buddy went down the steps to investigate the newcomer.

"Ready. Fire!"

As another blast echoed through the valley, Buddy ran around the camper twice and then stopped at the station wagon's rear window, his tail wagging furiously. He barked an invitation for the Irish setter to play a game of chase. But the setter, tempted though she was, remained steadfast in the vehicle and watched with envious brown eyes as Buddy chased his large fluffy, white tail and retreated to the porch to rejoin Holly.

The hot sultry afternoon wore on, the humidity intensified, and Holly continued to wait impatiently on the front porch of the cabin. At four o'clock some of the crowd began to drift to their cars and slowly make their way around the crowded circle to the main road exit. Holly, vastly relieved that the festivities were finally at an end, gave up her vigil for the late-arriving dignitary and nodded to Buddy that at last their sentence was over.

Buddy excitedly ran out to the station wagon and woofed again for the Irish to join them, but the loyal setter remained as she had been commanded by her owner. As Holly and Buddy started around the side of the cabin, the confined dog bounded into the back of the wagon, rested her chin against the seat, her soft liquid brown eyes following their departure.

"Sorry, Irish," Holly called, "but at least your arrogant master picked a nice shady spot to park."

For a moment Holly thought about the man who had taken the guest of honor's parking place without even asking. *Oh, he was more than arrogant. He was insolent, impertinent, and uppity and...* she smiled ruefully to herself, *and disarmingly handsome.* In fact, she admitted to herself, he was probably the most handsome man she had ever seen, with that chiseled face, and those broad shoulders which had to be the result of a lot of work or exercise. His was not a boyish handsomeness, either....

"Well, Holly Scott," she interrupted herself aloud as she and Buddy ran up the hill behind the cabin, "enough of that. Besides, that's the way handsome men usually act. With any luck, I'll never see that man again. Scarlett O'Hara indeed!"

They crossed the trail and ran into the densely wooded area beyond. Buddy ran ahead toward the quarry, but Holly called him back.

"Come on, boy. This way. We'd better stay off the trails today with this mob here."

They skirted the far side of the ridge and made their way to a little-used trail known only to the two of them, an unmarked trail that Holly knew her father wouldn't want her to use if he knew. He had warned her many times about the limestone sinks that were a real threat of danger to anyone who dared walk unmarked trails.

Ten minutes later Holly and Buddy were at a small glen on the banks of Roupe's Creek far below the furnaces. Holly called it her "hidin' place," a name she had taken from a childhood story. The glen was a shaded bend in the creek where the water oaks grew close to the bank and shaded a small inlet. Small graceful dogwoods skirted the creek and in the spring dotted the banks with white blossoms. Large rocks, seemingly set for the precise purpose of sunning, jutted out into the water.

At five o'clock the sun was already dropping behind the trees, casting faint shadows across Roupe's Creek. This place and time of day always made Holly reflective. She thought of it as the time that God had made for rest and preparation for another day.

Buddy cannonballed into the water, flying out almost into the middle of the swimming area. Holly removed her jeans and shirt, revealing a royal blue two-piece bathing suit, and dove from a large rock with sylphlike grace.

The minutes flew by until there were no more lacy spangles shimmering on the water and the glen grew

14

cool and deep green. The woods filled with dusky shadows.

"We'd better be on our way home, Buddy, or Daddy will be home before us, tired and hungry."

The girl and her dog raced through the woods. Buddy ran ahead, but now and then he doubled back to keep pace with Holly. They left the trail behind the cabin, ran down the hill and entered through the back door.

"Holly?" Her father's voice came from the front porch.

"Yes, Daddy," she answered breathlessly, as she automatically hooked the screen door just as she did every evening.

"Holly, we have guests for supper," John Scott called. "Come on out and meet them."

"Oh, no," she whispered aloud, thinking that the leftover ham she had planned to make into sandwiches would never stretch for guests. Why only last night her father had said that he couldn't wait until the ceremony was over and things were back to normal. But it was just like him to bring an unexpected guest or two for supper.

"I should have known," she sighed softly. Then she thought of something even worse than the leftover ham. What if Mr. Big from the Department of Interior had arrived after all and her father had invited him and his wife to supper? Her final concern was one she had been trying to suppress lately. She hoped no one had noticed today that her father seemed a bit tired. It was true that he had slowed down some, but he was still the best park superintendent in the whole world.

"Holly,..." John Scott's voice brought Holly back to the present problem, that of supper.

"I'll be out in a minute, Daddy," she called, looking

down at her damp clothes and dirty feet. She knew her hair completed the untidy picture.

"Holly!..." The inflection in her father's voice this time was one he hadn't used many times in her life, and she knew she had better make her appearance immediately even if she didn't look very presentable. She could change before supper. She slipped out the front door with Buddy at her heels.

Buddy wagged his tail in delight at the unexpected visitors while Holly stopped in her tracks. There on her porch, in her swing, with the beautiful mahogany Irish setter obediently at his feet, sat the tall, insolent stranger. A quick glance told her he had still not moved the station wagon and camper.

She stood there in her rumpled jeans and damp shirt, painfully aware of how she must look. The stranger rose from the swing to tower over her, a full head taller than her father, with shoulders that had no right to be that wide. He smiled the same slightly mocking smile as he had when she demanded that he not park in the reserved place. Eyes the pure blue of the early Tannehill morning sky looked at her with veiled laughter from beneath dark brows.

"This is Holly, my daughter," her father said with undisguised pride in his voice but a disapproving glance at her wet clothes and bare feet. She suddenly remembered what her father had said when she took off the dress she had worn to church that morning. "Holly, you could keep on that dress; there's going to be a lot of important people here today." But she, in rebellion against the crowds and disturbance, had pulled her oldest jeans and shirt from the closet and put them on. Now she regretted her lack of foresight.

"Seems you two didn't have time to get acquainted when he arrived," John Scott said.

16

She tried to compose herself, but something about the tall stranger standing there impeccable and cool in a tailored suit, which must have cost a fortune, while everyone else at Tannehill had wilted in the intense September heat, made her irritation increase.

"Well, we did exchange a few words while he was parking...in a reserved parking place."

Then almost before the words were out of her mouth, she knew that she had fallen into a trap. She knew exactly what her father's next words were going to be.

"Holly, this is our guest of honor, the representative from the United States Department of Interior, Mr. Luke Westford."

Chapter Two

"Mr. Westford." A simple acknowledgement was all Holly could manage to utter and she forced herself to muster up a little nod to go with it. And when Luke Westford extended his hand there was nothing she could do except place her fingers into his.

"Miss Scott," he said in a tone Holly was certain he used on members of Congress, and he inclined his head at an angle she was positive he usually reserved for foreign dignitaries. He didn't hold her hand a bit longer than was absolutely necessary, but Holly felt as if it had been an eternity.

As John Scott observed the two, he somehow felt he was seeing his daughter for the first time in his life. The magic current in the air between Luke Westford and Holly made John suddenly aware that his daughter was an attractive woman. Strange that he hadn't noticed before just how womanly she was becoming. He looked from Holly to Luke and back again, taking in the damp clothes clinging to a figure which was no longer tomboyish.

"Daddy, I'm sure Mr. Westford has important invitations for tonight and I certainly wouldn't want us to stand in his way. I thought there was a special reception in his honor."

Luke looked at Holly, his blue eyes darkened by the shadows that had overlaid the valley. "I'll be pleased to accept your father's invitation, Miss Scott—that is, if it won't inconvenience you. I'd rather spend a quiet evening at Tannehill than attend the reception. I've already extended my regrets."

Holly's only choice was to be gracious about the matter. Her father saved her from a direct answer.

"Holly, would you put on the coffee?" he asked, and as she turned to go back into the house he added, "and you might just get out of those wet clothes, too."

"Yes, Daddy," she answered, and turned, and fled into the house. In record time the coffee was perking in the old tin pot, and she hurried into the cabin's tiny bathroom.

She quickly showered and washed her hair. She took a clean pair of jeans and shirt from the bureau drawer. She certainly wasn't putting on a dress now. Her wet corn silk mane she braided into two plaits and secured the ends with the first ribbons she pulled from a box on her bureau. If she had bothered to glance in the mirror she might have seen that the scraps of rose ribbons reflected the peach bloom on her skin and that the severe hair style revealed her perfectly shaped oval face.

She slipped her feet into tan sandals, then kicked them off. "I won't be intimidated into wearing shoes, either," she whispered to herself. She hastily blotted the dampness from the ends of her braids one last time and returned to the kitchen.

She looked into the refrigerator with a sigh, then decided the ham would go further made into salad and spread on thick slices of dark bread. Tangy tomatoes,

19

peeled and sliced, from the vines just outside the kitchen door, and tall cool glasses of iced tea spiked with lemon wedges were all she could provide on such short notice. *That'll just have to do,* she thought. After all, it wasn't as if she had invited Mr. Luke Westford for supper. She took the large pot of Tannehill stew she had made for Buddy from the refrigerator and put it on the stove to warm.

As she poured the coffee into mugs, she wondered why she had never noticed the chip out of the handle of the cream pitcher before. Then she chided herself because she had allowed their arrogant guest to make her feel so inadequate. She carried the tray of coffee to the front porch and placed it on the lattice table. For a brief moment she thought about just letting the men serve themselves, but as angry as she was, her sense of southern hospitality wouldn't let her.

"Sugar or cream, Mr. Westford?" she asked, too politely, keeping her eyes on the tray.

"Black, thank you, Miss Scott," he answered in a voice that had no right to be so smooth and velvety while she was so agitated. She supposed she ought to be thankful he hadn't told her father about their earlier meeting and the way she had acted, but she felt more antagonistic than grateful.

Turning the cup so her fingers wouldn't touch his, she handed Luke Westford his coffee. She didn't notice the strange expression in her father's eyes as she handed him the other mug, and with a reminder that supper was only a few minutes away, she went back into the house.

As she crossed the living room into the kitchen, she looked at the cabin. It had never seemed so small before, not even when other guests had stayed over. It had always been just the right size for the three of them—including Buddy.

The cabin was a typical homestead house constructed in the 1800's. It contained only a small living room, a small bedroom on the back, which adjoined a tiny kitchen, a small room off the living room which served as Holly's bedroom, and a bath added to the original design. Like the other cabins at Tannehill, it had been carefully taken apart, labeled, and moved to the park where it was reassembled board by board.

Although the cabin was rustic outside, inside it was warm and cheerful, a testimony to Holly's handiwork. A braided rug in shades of brown, buff and orange covered the dark wood floor. Twin rockers were drawn near the rough stone fireplace. To the right of the stonework, a latch hook hanging depicting brown and cocoa pines against a beige background was suspended by a braided cord. The rockers flaunted matching latch hook pillows.

Across the living room a high-backed early American couch was flanked by small tables. The muted orange and rust floral pattern of the couch was repeated in globe lamps that lit the room. Osnaburg curtains gathered from dark decorator rods were tied back to admit the early evening light.

Against the back wall, a small five-tiered etagere stood respectfully, affirming the love that John and Rebecca had shared. The family Bible rested on the bottom shelf, and beside it stood a small wedding portrait of the couple. Mementos dotted the shelves. On the top, a photograph of a beautiful young woman was enclosed in a simple black frame, evidence that Holly Scott looked remarkably like her mother.

The bedrooms were small but charming, the focal point of each, a quilt that had either been handmade

21

or inherited by Rebecca Scott. John Scott's four-poster was covered with a quilt pieced in the "double wedding ring" pattern, a wedding present made by Rebecca's grandmother.

The saucy "Dutch Girls" on Holly's bed was a quilt divided by pale green strips, which matched the dust ruffle and Priscilla curtains. Three impertinent Dutch girls flirted from the frames of individual ruffled pillows banked against the brass headboard. An old bureau topped with a revolving oval mirror, and a table serving as a desk completed the small room. The faded mirror reflected a white ceramic Lenox vineyard box decorated with gold grape leaves.

One end of the tiny bath was filled with a white clawfoot tub, which shared a home with pristine white fixtures. In the far corner, a luxuriant peace plant sat regally on a white, three-legged fern stand.

In spite of her displeasure at the cabin's size, Holly could see nothing that she could do to make the cabin more presentable. It was no problem to keep such a small house clean. The floors were always spotless and the furniture always glossed with wax, which filled the house with the fragrance of lemon blossoms.

It's our home, little or not, she thought resentfully, *and he can like it or not.* But she felt a contrary twinge as she remembered her mother's best dishes were packed away because of the limited cabinet space in the kitchen. She told herself it didn't matter as she covered the kitchen table with a fresh cloth and pulled the plain white everyday plates from the shelf.

"Supper's ready," she called. She heard Luke Westford command his dog, Brandy, to stay on the porch. Then the familiar creak of the spring on the screen door announced that the two men had come inside. Her father asked Luke Westford if he wanted to wash up before supper. Holly was uneasy knowing that Luke Westford's expensive coat and tie were probably slung over the front room rocker while he was in their bathroom preparing to eat supper at their table.

Luke dominated the tiny kitchen as the three of them stood around the little table with its red-checked tablecloth and cane back chairs.

"Mr. Westford," she motioned to the chair on her father's right and she took the seat across the table so it would be easy for her to serve the food. But before she could be seated, Luke had stepped to her side and pulled out the chair for her just as if they were dining at the largest mansion in all of Alabama.

The seating arrangement wasn't the best after all, for every time Holly looked up, she found her own hazel eyes pulled toward the vivid blue sharpness of Luke Westford's gaze—unless she deliberately tried to look at something else.

The delicious aroma of Tannehill stew filled the cabin, and Luke cast a quick glance at the big pot on the stove.

"Buddy's supper," John Scott explained and, as Luke's face took on an expression of doubt, he continued, "Eats like a king, that dog does, and sometimes—if I'm lucky—Holly makes enough for me." He laughed. "It's a mighty tasty stew. Holly got the recipe out of some book she read."

"Do you read a lot, Miss Scott?" Luke asked in a tone that seemed to Holly to imply she didn't look like the scholarly type.

"Some, Mr. Westford," she answered, forcing herself to look directly into those cool blue eyes she felt were secretly mocking her.

"Humph! Some, indeed," her father interjected. "Why all that girl ever thinks about is books and reading when she isn't running the hills with Buddy." And without giving either Holly or Luke a chance to reply to that, he added, "Let's return thanks."

The three of them bowed their heads while John Scott thanked God for the food that graced the table and for the beauty of the day. His voice revealed to Luke Westford something that Holly already knew—his love for Tannehill.

Though Holly had a hearty appetite after swimming, Luke ate more than she and her father together. The big plate of sandwiches disappeared in record time and when Luke said he had enjoyed the meal, Holly knew that he meant it.

During supper Luke and John discussed the park service and forestry conservation and had a few laughs over some of the bloopers made during the furnace-tapping ceremony. Listening to Luke's interesting conversation, Holly forgot to be angry and she realized her father was thoroughly enjoying himself and their visitor.

Why, thought Holly, *I haven't heard Daddy laugh like this in a long time,* and then she wondered why she hadn't noticed it sooner. When had that subtle change come over him? But her nagging concern was lost in the beauty of Luke Westford's voice and the pleasure of her father's laughter.

After the meal John Scott rose from the table and asked Luke to join him on the front porch for a smoke. But Luke declined.

"I've got to see to the Irish," he said with a smile that slashed across his face for a brief moment, revealing teeth which were strong, white, and even. When he turned to thank Holly for the meal, he saw that she had already filled two large red plastic bowls with

24

crunchy nuggets of dog food and generous helpings of Tannehill stew.

"Your Brandy was invited, too," Holly said, smiling in spite of herself as she set the two bowls down on the linoleum. She went to the front door to call the dogs. Buddy bounded into the house and went for one of the bowls, but Brandy stayed fast at the door with a regretful look on her face.

"Mr. Westford, please call your Irish in for supper," Holly said, holding the screen door open until Luke's voice brought the dog racing through the house and into the kitchen, where she began to eat from the other bowl.

"There's plenty of stew on the stove," Holly admonished the dogs, "so you just ask for more if you want it." She looked up to find Luke's eyes on her. His expression disconcerted her. She stared back at him, momentarily caught off guard.

"Sorry," Luke said, "it's just that I don't find many people who talk to dogs like that. You sounded as if you really thought they could understand what you said."

She tilted her chin in that defiant gesture he had seen on their first encounter. "Buddy is more than just a dog to me. And so is your Brandy and all the creatures of the park. They're special—they're friends to me."

"I wasn't being critical. Brandy is a good friend of mine."

Buddy interrupted to bark for seconds and Holly turned her attention to the pot of stew on the stove. She filled Buddy's bowl again and added two cups to the rapidly disappearing serving in front of Brandy. Then she began to clear the table.

"To make amends for having an uninvited guest for

dinner—er, supper, I'd like to help you with the dishes, Miss Scott."

Holly's eyes widened at that remark. "Daddy invited you," she said, but before she could protest further Luke had taken charge of her kitchen. John Scott, who had stepped into the living room to make room for the dogs in the kitchen, raised his eyebrows and turned and walked out on the porch. He sat down in the old rocker and thoughtfully tamped the tobacco into his pipe.

"I'll wash and you dry and put things away," Luke said as he stoppered the sink, poured dishwasher liquid into the porcelain basin and added hot water just as if he had done it a thousand times before. He rolled up his expensive white shirt sleeves and revealed muscular forearms. His wrist was banded with a plain gold watch which Holly figured would cost more than her father's salary for a month.

"Your watch,…" Holly exclaimed as he plunged his hands into the water and began to wash the dishes.

"Waterproof," he commented briefly as he flipped a plate and washed the back side.

Holly looked at this strange man making himself at home in her kitchen, standing there tall and elegant in his tailored pants and his soft white shirt with the sleeves rolled up. She knew she would be glad when he was gone because she didn't like the way he made her feel.

"Humph,…" John Scott cleared his throat from his vantage point in the doorway. He had walked back into the house unnoticed. For the second time in one evening he felt that his daughter and Luke Westford were in a world of their own and that he was watching a drama in which he had no part. "Humph…I think I'll walk over to the store and check with Charlie to be sure everything went all right today."

"But, Daddy—" Holly began.

"I'll be back before you get the dishes washed and we'll sit on the porch a spell." He turned amid Holly's protest and left the kitchen.

Buddy barked for Holly to unhook the screen, then he pushed the door open and bounded into the back yard. He turned and looked back for Brandy, who was cleaning one last morsel from her bowl.

"Stay in the yard, Brandy," Luke commanded as she went to join Buddy.

"Buddy knows not to leave the yard when the park is crowded," Holly said reassuringly.

Now Holly was alone with Luke in the house. She wondered why she had never been so aware of being alone with anyone before. Charlie had been to supper and helped her with the dishes before, but he had never made her feel one bit like she was feeling at the moment. Just what was it about Luke Westford that intimidated and antagonized her?

They worked in silence for a few minutes, and she had to admit that he was quite efficient in the kitchen for a man. Then, she reflected, he was probably quite efficient at a lot of things or he wouldn't be such a Mr. Big Shot at the Interior Department.

"Mr. Westford," Holly paused momentarily, summoned up her courage, turned and looked him directly in the eyes. "You could have told me who you were this afternoon, you know, instead of just leading me down the garden path and letting me say all those things." She shut the door to the cabinet harder than she intended and the glasses tinkled a reprimand.

"Whoa, Scarlett," he drawled. "I tried to tell you who I was but you wouldn't listen. Do you always shoot first and ask questions later?" He glanced down at her from his superior height with a mock serious expression on his face that exaggerated his fake southern accent.

"You still could have told me," she insisted, as she placed the plates in the cabinet and put the last of the dirty dishes on the counter at Luke's right.

"There wasn't time to argue and besides, I didn't want to spoil your little drama—that fire and brimstone speech complete with southern drawl. I half expected to see a pink ribbon tied around your toe." He finished the last dish and let the water out. Then he rinsed his hands and dried them on the hand towel Holly kept hooked through the refrigerator door handle.

"Mr. Westford, I've always thought that Washington officials were supposed to be masters of tact, but I fail to see that you have any. None of this would have happened if you'd been on time." Her smile belied her accusation.

"You have a point there," he said as he watched her stand on bare tiptoes to put the old cream and sugar set on the top shelf. She stretched gracefully, her small feet arched like a ballet dancer's.

She turned and looked at him as he continued to survey her slender form.

"Why did you leave your wife at home and bring your dog?" she asked using her very best drawl. *I can't just let him look at me like that and get away with it,* she thought.

"When was the last time you had a spanking?" The wintry blue of Luke's eyes was as chilling as the tone of his voice.

Holly stared at Luke, a flush of embarrassment coloring her cheeks. She had never felt so immature and gauche.

28

Luke's voice was softer and the wintry look faded from his eyes when he replied, "I don't have a wife, and the couple who looks after my place is visiting their son, so I brought Brandy with me."

"I haven't had a spanking since Mother died. I guess Daddy just couldn't bring himself to do it, even when I needed one." She smiled mischievously, "Besides, Daddy says he likes me just the way I am because I add a little spice to his life."

"Mostly pepper," Luke commented dryly. Then he quickly added, "Since the Civil War has been over for a hundred years, why don't we call a truce?"

"Truce," agreed Holly, "but for your information it was the War Between the States."

"Add cinnamon to the pepper," Luke laughed.

"Mr. Westford, why did you come to supper here to-night when all those fancy invitations had been extended to you?" Holly knew she was treading on dangerous ground again, but it was a question she might never get the chance to ask later.

"Not to give you a bad time because of this afternoon, if that's what you're thinking. I just didn't feel like attending that reception and when your father suggested a quiet evening, I took him up on it."

Holly looked speculatively at him. "Now you don't look a bit like you're not up to facing a reception this evening—or any evening."

"Well,..." Luke mused for a moment, "your father invited Brandy to come along."

"Oh," Holly said, taken aback that anyone besides herself would turn down a fancy invitation because of a dog. She led the way through the living room to the porch.

They went out into the soft Alabama night. The woods were filled with the chirping of crickets and adorned by the lilting glimmers of fireflies. The moon had cast mother-of-pearl patterns across the park circle in front of the house.

"Won't you sit and wait for Daddy?" Holly offered, determined to be a good hostess and observe their truce during her last moments with Luke Westford.

"Thank you, Miss Scott, but I want to get an early start in the morning and there are still a lot of things I have to do. Like moving out of your…reserved parking place over to my camp site."

The retort that rose to her lips was stifled when she saw that he had picked up his coat and tie as they had crossed the living room. He stepped down to the second step and Holly saw that he was still a little taller than she. The light from the living room fell across the strong lines of his face and she looked directly into the depths of the blue eyes, which were now almost level with her own. The sensation was like the first time she ever saw the ocean—blue, deep, and dangerous, as if the whole world could be reflected there if she dared look close enough to see it.

"Thanks for the delicious dinner—er, supper, and a very interesting evening, though not as quiet as I had anticipated." He extended his hand and for the second time that evening she put her fingers into his.

He's making fun of me again, she thought, *but I can be nice just another moment and then he'll be gone.* But when their fingers touched that feeling was swept away and replaced by a moment of regret. Luke Westford would be on his way early in the morning and when she came home from her classes, the park would be just like it was before—serene and peaceful with no trace of Luke Westford and his Irish setter.

"You're welcome," she said and it sounded so much like she meant it that Luke's eyebrows raised a fraction.

"I'll see your father in the morning before I get started," he said, glancing in the direction of the store.

"I'll tell him."

"Good night, Holly." Their eyes met for a brief moment before he turned and hooked his coat over his shoulder. He whistled to Brandy who obediently appeared from the shadows and heeled on his left.

"Good-bye, Luke" she said softly, half to him and half to herself.

Without so much as a backward glance he backed the big blue Catalina and camper out of the drive and drove around the big circle and pulled into his camp site.

Holly switched off the living room light and returned to the swing to enjoy the Alabama night. She watched a moonlight ballet under the pines. Phantom shadows were the danseurs and fragile moonbeams were their graceful partners. But more than once her eyes strayed from the beauty of the nocturnal dance to the lights visible in a camper parked across the creek.

She conceded that she would think of Luke Westford in the days to come. It would take more than a day to erase the impact of a man like that from Tannehill. But, she reminded herself again, she was glad that he was gone. Yes, tomorrow when she came home from classes, everything would be back to normal.

"Holly, tomorrow's a school day," her father's voice jerked her from her reverie. She had been so absorbed thinking about Luke Westford she hadn't even heard him come home from the store.

"You don't need to remind me of that, Daddy," she smiled ruefully. Although Holly liked her courses in history at the university, there were times that she longed for the freedom and splendor of the woods.

"Well, to bed then, young lady," he spoke quietly, affection filtering into his voice. It was clear that Holly was the pride and joy of his life. Holly and Tannehill—that about summed it up for John Scott.

"Daddy," Holly spoke as she rose from the swing and walked toward the door, "Mr. Westford said he couldn't wait. He had to be going because he wanted to get an early start in the morning."

"He mentioned that to me, but I suspect it's just as much because of this morning as tomorrow morning." John Scott settled himself in his rocker, took out his pipe, and gave it a rap on the rocker armrest.

Holly opened the screen door, then let it close. "This morning?"

"I wouldn't have known myself if Charlie hadn't heard it on the radio. Westford ain't the kind of man to tell something like that. Seems there was a wreck on the interstate and he stopped to help. Smashed the window of a car in order to pull an injured man out. Luke got his shoulder and upper arm cut up enough for stitches. It's a good thing he stopped since the car went up right after he got the man out."

"Went up?"

"Exploded, Holly."

She stood very still; all the words she had flung at Luke about being late came back to her and raced about in her mind.

"Somebody at the emergency room recognized his name from reading about the celebration plans. That's how it got on the news. Charlie came down to the furnace and told me just before Westford arrived."

"Was he hurt much, Daddy?"

"Enough so that he didn't feel up to that reception. That's why I invited him to have supper with us when he mentioned he was tired. Can't figure him feeling up to washing dishes though."

"Good night, Daddy," Holly said as she went into the house. She wanted to be alone and sort out the events of the day. Something was wrong and she didn't know what it was. She owed Luke Westford an apology alright, but there was another little piece of the puzzle still missing.

She sat on the edge of the bed in the dark and slowly loosened her hair from the confines of the braids.

"Daddy," she called, "I owe Mr. Westford an apology. I said some rather rude things because he was late today."

"We all thought the same, Holly. Don't worry about it."

"Maybe I'd better get up a little early in the morning and speak to him about it."

"There's no need to bother him in the morning, Holly. You can speak your piece tomorrow afternoon." John Scott got up from his rocker and let Buddy into the house. Then he walked to the edge of the porch and leaned against the rough post, looking out across the park circle

"Tomorrow afternoon? Don't you remember, Daddy, he said he would be getting an early start?"

"Not for home, Holly. He's going into town to buy groceries and check in at the local commission office."

"He's staying over!"

"Yes, Holly, Mr. Westford is going to be here a while and I told him you'd show him around the park after school."

Holly sank back into the bed as she whispered to Buddy. "Well, he did it again. Led me down the garden path again. He just let me say all those things he knew I'd be sorry for later." She reached out for the velvet smoothness of Buddy's head. "Like Scarlett O'Hara said, Buddy, 'Tomorrow is another day.' "

Her eyes closed but before she drifted to sleep, she admitted to herself that she was glad Luke Westford would be a part of her tomorrow.

Chapter Three

Charlie had to blow the horn three times before Holly finally came out of the cabin. The smooth line of his forehead wrinkled a little; Holly wasn't usually late.

Even after the second blast of the horn, Holly slowly fastened the buckle straps of the lattice-patterned, stacked-heel sandals she had finally selected from her closet shelf. Her mind was definitely not concerned with responding to Charlie's honking. She was preoccupied with the idea that her father was deliberately throwing her into the company of Luke Westford.

"Suffering sciatica, Holly. It's ten after seven!" Charlie's voice admonished her small transgression, but his eyes admiringly forgave, taking in her ivory-and-tan striped pullover and the neat tan slacks.

"Oh, Charlie," Holly protested as she tossed her books into the back seat and settled in beside him. "Not W. C. Fields at seven in the morning."

"Seven-ten," he corrected, shifting the red Mustang into low. "Who would you prefer at seven in the morning—Groucho?"

"I think I'd prefer peace and quiet," Holly lamented, pretending she hadn't understood the double-entendre directed at her disposition

"A beautiful, gorgeous day and you aren't satisfied. You want peace and—"

"The most beautiful thing about today, Charlie, is that yesterday is over," Holly interrupted him.

"You, too, huh?" Charlie gave up and joined Holly's lead. "I thought the park would never clear out last night. At least you could go to bed at a decent hour. I didn't close the store until almost midnight."

"Well, if it makes you feel any better, I couldn't sleep," she rebutted.

"You don't *look* like you lost any sleep, Holly," Charles grumbled, running a hand through his thatch of curls.

"Lack of sleep didn't do that to your hair, Charlie," Holly baited him, trying to get her thoughts away from her father and Luke Westford. "It was Mother Nature."

"Mother Nature gave it all to you, Flower Belle. 'What a euphonious appellation—easy on the ears and a banquet for the eyes.' " Charles lapsed into his favorite pastime, spouting "Fieldisms."

"Charlie," Holly laughed, sliding down in the seat to rest her head on its back, "not at seven-thirty."

Charlie, not to be outdone, launched into an account of yesterday's incidents—the ice cream machine that stuck and made the world's largest ice cream cone, the lost twins who gave conflicting information, and the coffee he had perked without grounds.

Charlie Bradley and Holly had always commuted together to the university. They had been friends since elementary school days and it had just been understood that when they went to the university, it would be together. Charles worked part-time at the Tannehill camp store, and when Holly caught up with all the odd jobs around the park her father assigned her to do, she usually went down to the store and helped out there. On slow days, she and Charlie sometimes had an opportunity for a little studying together. Every quarter they had managed to have at least one class together.

It was hard to tell which end of Charlie's hair was attached, but the sun-bleached curls suited his outgoing personality and friendly smile. His athletic frame was usually attired in jeans and a pullover shirt.

Charles's most endearing characteristic was his zany, irrepressible sense of humor. It was very difficult to get mad at him, and virtually impossible to stay mad at him. He would invariably retaliate with a line from a wounded, dying hero in an old movie of the twenties or thirties. If that didn't do it, his smile would.

"Holly, what's the matter with you?" Charles asked.

"The matter with me?"

"I asked you what time that guy from the Interior Department finally arrived and you never even heard me."

"I don't exactly know, Charlie. It was real late." Holly was surprised at her unwillingness to share her encounter with Luke Westford with Charlie. Any other time, they would have made jokes about it, interspersing the tale with peals of laughter.

"I thought you might come down to the store and talk while everyone was over at the ceremony," Charles's words were edged with disappointment.

"I knew you had enough extra help for the day, Charlie," Holly said, turning to retrieve her notebook from the back seat. "I think I'd better look over some notes," she said, flipping the book open, "I have an English exam."

Holly slowly crossed the athlete's walkway, the university's answer to Hollywood, where the handprints and cleated footprints of football heroes were immortalized in the concrete sidewalk. Any other time she would have enjoyed looking at the interesting indentions, but today her mind was on something else. She had to solve that nagging riddle of her father and Luke Westford.

At the library, her luck was no better. It was like a puzzle with a few missing pieces. She made a determined effort to study her English notes, but her mind restlessly returned to her father, then to Luke.

As the moments ticked by, her father slipped away from her thoughts and Luke Westford dominated the scene. She remembered the vivid blue of his eyes, the way he had taken over her kitchen, and the feelings that had surprised her when she had learned that he was not leaving Tannehill the next morning.

As Lynn Jackson, a friend from English class, stopped at the table to say hello, Holly noticed it was almost time for her exam. Then she looked at her notes. She was still on the first page.

In the middle of her English exam the hidden truth of the matter hit Holly. The professor jokingly said they had better do their best because it was their last chance—he was retiring at the end of the quarter. Then the whole thing just fell into place: Why, it wasn't that her father wanted her to be with Luke Westford, but rather he was afraid for some reason to be in the close proximity of the government representative!

Holly looked at the face of the professor, a face that was lined from years of teaching. Then she remembered the pinched look that seemed to have settled about her father's mouth lately. The slight droop of his once-erect body stood out vividly in her mind. *Why, he had just invented all those important things he had to do so Westford wouldn't discover that he wasn't feeling his best.*

Of course! That was the answer. She knew her father was just tired, but Luke Westford might not be so understanding. Holly clenched her slender fingers about the pen she was holding and stared at the mimeographed questions until the letters blurred as it dawned on her what might happen if Luke Westford thought her father couldn't handle his job. No matter that her father was employed by the Tannehill Commission—Westford obviously had some personal influence on the management of the park or he wouldn't have been asked to speak at the ceremony.

She knew then what she must do. She would stand between them. Her father had asked for her help, in a rather indirect way to be certain, and she would give it to him. Tannehill Park was her father's life and she would do anything she could to insure that no one took it away from him.

As for Westford—well, she would just have to grit her teeth and bear his arrogant presence. She would have to overcome that feeling of being intimidated when she was around him. She would fight the self-consciousness that had enveloped her last night. She wasn't a child and he had no right to make her feel like one.

Holly's thoughts were still in a turmoil when she met Charles at the car. No amount of his coaxing, however, would persuade her to share her problem.

"It's all the excitement and hubbub of yesterday, Charlie," she said for the third time as they turned into the park, "and I'm exhausted."

"Well, take a nap, then come on down to the store."

"I can't today, Charlie. I've got to show. .Mr. Westford around. Daddy's got something else he has to do." *Why*, she asked herself, *did I hesitate at his name?*

At that moment Holly saw Buddy waiting at the top of the bank beside the road, and at her request Charlie stopped the car and let her out so that she could walk the rest of the distance with her dog.

Holly and Buddy skirted up through the trees and crossed the road to the ridge behind the cabin. There was no time today to admire a wildflower or an unusually beautiful leaf. They hurried down the narrow path to the cabin. Although Buddy was obedient and the park was usually deserted on Monday afternoons, Holly and Buddy were obliged to avoid the inner park circle where leash signs were posted.

Voices from the front porch drifted through the house to the kitchen. Holly couldn't make out the words, but she recognized the unusually hearty laughter of her father and the low vibrant voice of Luke Westford. *No one could find fault with her father's sense of humor,* she thought, as she poured herself a glass of iced tea. A friendly burble from the coffee pot on the stove and sugar sprinkles on the table told her that she didn't need to offer her father or Luke Westford afternoon refreshments.

In only a matter of minutes she had showered and donned fresh jeans and shirt. She glanced briefly in the mirror atop the old bureau as she ran a comb through her hair and secured it at the base of her neck with a faded blue ribbon. She was oblivious to the perfect oval of her face, the bewitching beauty of her green eyes tilting ever so slightly at the corners, and the translucent quality of her skin which was flawless even in the brilliant Tannehill sunlight.

With an assumed confidence she went out the screen door and bent to kiss her father's lined cheek.

"Hi, Daddy," she whispered. Then, with reluctance, she turned and faced her father's companion.

"Good afternoon, Mr. Westford."

"Miss Scott," he returned, rising from the swing with as much sang-froid as he had had the night before, though he was attired in worn denim jeans and shirt. The shirt, a darker shade of blue, was rolled up two turns at the cuffs, just as his dress shirt sleeves had been when he had washed dishes the night before.

"I'll keep an eye on Brandy and Buddy while I finish my report," her father said, picking up a folder from the floor beside his rocker. "Ya'll better get started."

Holly cast an anxious glance at her father as she said good-bye and followed Luke Westford out to the blue Pontiac. She looked across the park at the litter left from yesterday's celebration and muttered, "People shouldn't be allowed in parks." Then she ran ahead and opened the door of the car, determined not to let Luke play the gallant gentleman.

Luke didn't speak until they were on the main road and then it was without so much as a glance in her direction.

"Parks were established for the pleasure of people, Holly," he said quietly.

"Well, sometimes people nearly make this place into a disaster area," she replied. "Did you see the park this morning before the men started to clean it up?"

"Yes, I saw it. But it's people who pay the taxes."

Holly fell silent for a moment, conceding that point without comment.

"It's just that some people are careless. I guess they don't think about what they're doing."

"Still, most people are fairly conscientious about parks," Luke persisted.

"I suppose you're right," Holly said, fully aware that

41

the majority of the visitors to Tannehill were respectful of the grounds.

"Have you lived at Tannehill long?" Luke inquired, shifting to a neutral subject.

"Since about a year after it opened," Holly said, "and I was born near here."

"Where?"

"It doesn't have a name—just here in the valley in a little house Daddy rented."

"And...." Luke prompted.

"And it was one of those winters when people were snowed in and there was no way to get to the hospital. After I was born Daddy went out in the woods and collected some holly and brought it to my mother. That's why she named me Holly."

"Your mother...?" Luke inquired softly.

"She had a hard time. I don't think she ever fully recovered. Daddy never talks about it much. Her health just went from bad to worse after that. She died when I was four." Holly's voice faded a little as she realized he was listening intently to her story.

"That sort of explains why you're so sensitive about the park, Holly. It's not just a park to you. It's home."

"Is that all it is to you, just a park?" her eyes clashed with his. She hadn't meant to talk to him like this, telling him about her childhood and sharing old memories as if he were a close friend. She felt forced into raising her defenses again.

"No, Holly. No park is just a park to me. They're not just beautiful scenery or natural resources. Parks are special to me, too."

"And...." It was her turn to prompt him.

Luke laughed at her obvious ploy, and in spite of herself, her bubbly laughter joined his.

"All right, Holly you asked for it." He raised his eyebrows a notch. "How about inspiration, revitalization, historical perspective, lore, and legends."

"You've got a real knack for words, but that comes natural to bureaucrats, doesn't it?" Holly spoke in jest, but she was glad that he had spoken as he had, glad that someone else felt a little bit the way she did about Tannehill.

"And you have a knack for making comments that rub like sandpaper against the grain."

"Turn right at the next road," she said politely, ignoring his last remark. "We're almost there."

A covered bridge loomed into view and Luke slowed the station wagon and turned off the main road. He pulled over to the shoulder and switched off the ignition. But instead of focusing his attention on the bridge, he turned to Holly and studied her young, intense face. Though her own eyes were fastened on the bridge, she could feel his eyes on her. The sensation made her know there was something about being in the same car with Luke Westford that she didn't want to analyze at that moment.

He turned in his seat and continued to look at her.

"Why did you agree to be my guide? I'm sure that your father could have found someone else. Someone who wanted to—"

"Oh, I wanted to," Holly interrupted.

"Then why be so contentious with me? You've taken exception to everything I've said this afternoon. You could have very easily told your father you didn't want to accompany me, or are you so obedient a daughter that you never think about disobeying your father's wishes?" There was a barb in his last statement and Holly suspected he was referring to her absence during the furnace re-firing ceremony.

"Why didn't you suggest someone else when

Daddy mentioned me for your guide, Mr. Westford?" she countered.

"Your father offered your services before I met you, Holly."

"If you're disappointed, why don't you ask for a replacement?" She didn't mean to say that and she regretted it instantly, but the words were out. She sat very still and held her breath. If he took her up on her challenge, she would have let her father down.

"No," he said slowly, his eyes narrowing slightly, "I'll just leave the decision up to you. Do you want to go back now and call it quits?"

"I never call anything quits," she retorted, shaking her head.

"I do believe I've seen one redeeming quality in you, Miss Scott, or is there a little bit of revenge hidden beneath that unsinkable facade?"

"Do you think I have any reason for revenge, Mr. Westford?" she asked with a touch of sticky southern sweetness in her voice.

"Does it matter? Most of the time revenge has no valid reason or motive."

"Does that matter? People still seek it."

He shook his head slightly, a faint smile hovering about his mouth. "Shall we just agree to be mutually tolerant of each other? Perhaps whatever it is about me that rubs you the wrong way won't work its way down to the quick before I'm finished here."

"That's fine with me," she agreed.

I'll just have to hold my temper, she lectured herself. Surely she could do that for her father's sake. One thing was certain—her father wasn't up to this trip they were making this afternoon and Luke Westford was too observant not to notice that all was not well with the park superintendent. It would destroy her father if the park board asked him to leave, or even if they thought he wasn't doing a good job. Whatever was wrong, it would soon pass. If only he were his old self, she wouldn't have to put up with Luke Westford.

"I'm going to get a closer look at the bridge," Luke said as he got out of the car.

She opened her door and ran across the leaves to catch up with his long strides. They entered the structure together, walking side by side, and again Holly was aware of just how tall he was. She barely reached to his shoulder. Suddenly she had the bizarre notion that his shoulder would be a mighty comfortable place to rest her head if she were in need of comfort. Then the hollow sounds of their footsteps inside the bridge brought her back to reality.

Luke studied the architectural structure of the bridge briefly, then turned to Holly.

"What courses are you taking in college?"

She was taken by surprise at his question and she stopped to search his face which was now obscure in the musty shadows of the bridge. In the dimness his head was a morion silhouette against the brilliance of the day at the end of the tunnel.

"Well...this quarter I'm taking history, English, and chemistry."

"And your major?"

"History," she said, wondering if he were really interested, then deciding that he had just picked a safer topic of conversation than the park.

"And after college?"

"I'm going to teach. I'll get my certificate next August when I graduate."

"That's a rewarding occupation, Holly, even though it's probably a tough one these days."

"I suppose every job has its problems, even yours."

"Even mine," he agreed. "But the good times weigh the balance, like spending this time at Tannehill."

"Exactly what is your job, Mr. Westford?" she asked.

"Jack-of-all-trades," he declared with a low laugh. "I'm working with state and local agencies in the Midwest Region in their effort to develop outdoor recreation facilities."

And you probably have a lot of clout with the state park commission, Holly thought. *Just how dangerous are you, Luke Westford?* Holly wanted to know more about this man.

"And before that?"

"I spent several years working with historical preservation in D.C."

That partially answered Holly's questions. He was very dangerous. He could be the friend of anybody—congressmen, state legislators, even the governor.

"Is that how you wrangled this invitation?" she ventured pointedly, hoping she wasn't pressing her luck too far. However, at the look that crossed his face, she quickly tried another question.

"Why the shift from Washington?"

"Closer to home."

"Where's home?" Holly decided there was a distinct advantage in asking the questions.

"Iowa. An area much like the one where you were born, too sparcely settled to have a name." He moved to inspect a timber in the bridge and shifted the conversation back to her.

"Your father mentioned you commute to the university with Charles Bradley. Is he your steady boyfriend?"

"What is this? Twenty questions?" Holly bantered, wondering why his inquiry should make her feel uneasy.

46

"I withdraw the question," he amended, his brows faintly lifting.

Holly answered it anyway.

"Charlie and I have been friends for as long as I can remember. He's worked at the park several years. We even went to grade school together. We've commuted together to the university for three years."

"That university's an excellent school, Holly. And you have a great football team."

"Yes!" Holly quickly agreed.

Luke inspected another timber and changed the subject.

"Tell me about all those books you read that your father mentioned last night."

"This *is* twenty questions!" Holly laughed. "Those are the books I buy for a bargain on Trade Days."

"When are Trade Days?"

"Every third weekend of the month from March to November. The park is filled with arts, crafts, folk music, and, of course, thousands of people. Sometimes as many as four thousand of them and they carelessly—"

"We're not going through that topic again, Holly," Luke interrupted. "Now, about those books."

She smiled in spite of herself. "Once I bought a book of veterinary medicine for just a dollar. The back was off but all the information was there, and I have some books on trees and plant life and soil conservation and—"

"You don't look like a college senior, Holly," Luke interrupted again, "but I approve of your reading material."

"I'm twenty-two...almost," she added quickly.

"How...almost?" he challenged, as he looked down at her, a flicker of a smile tugging at the corners of his mouth.

"Well,..." She hesitated a moment, lifting her eyes to his. They had moved into the light again and she had the same peculiar sensation of the ocean that she had experienced on the steps the night before, except this time instead of being calm, it was like ocean breakers crashing against craggy rocks. "Nine months," she finished.

Luke Westford laughed then, and Holly, glad for the respite, smiled. She was strangely aware that his laughter warmed her. It gave her almost as much pleasure as hearing her father's laughter last night. But before she could examine why, Luke spoke.

"We'd better be on our way, Holly, before we have another argument."

The giant sinkhole yawned in the Alabama hillside, its gaping mouth forming a hundred-and-twenty foot crater. The diameter at the widest part of the collapsed area was five hundred feet. Rainfall had slowly eroded the soil beneath the surface of the ground until it became an area of perched groundwater. The overburdened surface eventually collapsed, forming a crater which had made national news.

The parking area where Luke parked the car was several hundred yards from the sinkhole. They walked the narrow trail single file with Holly leading the way. The earth on either side of the trail was dotted with slanting trees, sinking stumps, and signs of shifting earth and underground streams. As they neared the hole, the spongy areas and small crevices increased.

At the rim of the crater, they peered down into the circular cavern. The bottom was filled with muddy water and a few scrubby trees had pushed up from fissures toward the sun.

"The old folks say there's no bottom to it," Holly

said, glancing up at Luke who stood beside her on the rim of the sink.

"Do you believe them?" he asked, a mock note of seriousness in his low vibrant voice.

"No," she laughed. "I figured it all out the first time I saw it."

"What did you 'figure'?" Luke asked, mimicking her informal expression.

"Oh, that you couldn't very well fall clear through the earth and out the other side because then you'd be falling up." She spoke mischievously, ignoring his derision of her colloquialism.

"You do a lot of 'figuring,' don't you, Holly?"

"Well, I already 'figured' out that you're laughing at the way I talk!" She tilted her chin up in that little defiant gesture that was to haunt him in the days to come.

Luke looked at her very seriously for a moment, his eyes the gleaming blue of Arctic seas. "I wasn't laughing at you, Holly. Just teasing you a little."

"I guess that's all right, provided you can take a little yourself." She didn't give him a chance to answer that. "There's a small sink just over there. The Geological Service says it may be bigger than this one when it goes, maybe three hundred feet deep and just as wide. Would you like to see it?" Then without waiting for him to answer, she started around the rim toward the path on the other side that led to the small sink. As she turned off the rim, she glanced back.

Luke Westford was kneeling on one knee, one hand on the very edge of the rim, his other hand holding a small sapling that curved toward the sink.

Holly's heart hammered rapidly as she remembered the injury he had received only yesterday in that freeway accident. She hurried back along the rim and dropped to her knees beside him, clutching at his free arm and pulling him back from the chasm.

"Luke!" she exclaimed, remembering guiltily how she had hurried up the slope when he had obviously been in no condition to go that fast.

He looked at her, the frosty blue of his eyes replaced by a surprised expression.

"Is...is it your wound?" she asked anxiously, holding tightly to his arm. She saw that he held some dirt in his fingers. Had he been about to fall forward into the sink and caught himself? "Does it hurt terribly?"

"Well, it does ache some," he said, looking down at her, the surprised expression gradually changing to a different one.

"Lean back against this tree until you catch your breath," she cautioned, turning him by the arm until his back was near a tree large enough to bear his weight.

"It would be nice to rest for a moment," he agreed, resting against the tree and stretching his long legs into the path. He closed his eyes.

"Are you dizzy?" Holly asked anxiously, reaching for his hand and holding it tightly.

"No," he said, but he didn't open his eyes.

"Oh, you're just like Daddy. You wouldn't admit you were feeling poorly, even if you were dying. Maybe you'd better lie down."

"No," he said, "this is very comfortable."

Holly reached up and felt his brow. Her hand was cool and gentle.

He doesn't feel like a person about to faint, she thought. *His skin isn't a bit clammy*. On the contrary, Luke Westford's skin felt warm and vital, like silk stretched over steel. She drew her hand back, a little disturbed over the way it had made her feel to touch him. She tried to disengage the fingers of her other hand from his, but he held them tightly. She glanced at his face but his eyes were still closed.

Taking advantage of the moment, she looked closely at Luke Westford, at the strong brown column of his neck and the well-shaped head, at the dark hair that seemed edged in gold here and there in the sunlight that filtered through the trees, at the well-defined dark brows and the dark lashes that had tiny dashes of gold on the tips.

Just at that moment Luke opened his eyes and did a little survey of his own, which caused the color to rise in Holly's face. She somehow managed to release both her hand and eyes from his hold and stood to her feet. Luke was standing almost at the same time.

"Are you feeling better now?" she asked politely, fighting for composure, a bit disconcerted because he was the one who ought to be feeling uncomfortable.

"I feel fine," he assured her. "Shall we go?"

"If you're determined to go on," she said, unde-cided whether or not to insist they go back.

Holly walked beside Luke along the trail, on guard to extend a helping hand, still very concerned over the incident that had just occurred. They walked slowly around the sink, pausing at the path that went down from the rim. It was a short walk over to the other sink and another short climb to the top. The path narrowed so that it was impossible to walk together.

"Are you all right?" Holly asked, taking the lead.

"Yes," Luke assured her.

They made their way up the path slowly, Holly glancing back every few feet to be certain Luke was close behind her. *Strange,* she thought, *he seems to be climbing this hill easier than I am.*

As Holly reached the top of the path and looked

over into the sink, she saw a small white flower growing in a crevice about three feet below the rim. She leaned over to inspect the treasure she had discovered. Suddenly, Luke's arms were about her, pulling her back from the edge. Before she had time to protest, he had released her except for a firm grasp on her hand.

"You know better than that, Holly!" he said abruptly. "Your father was right. You do need looking after." There was a reprimand in his voice.

"I wasn't going to fall. I was only looking." The tone of his voice had made her feel five years old again and for some reason she didn't want to feel that way anymore, especially around Luke Westford. She tried to remove her hand from his. *He doesn't seem a bit weak,* she thought.

"That's what everyone thinks just before they have an accident, Holly. And, if you'll calm down, I'll be more than happy to turn you loose."

She tried once more to extricate herself from his hold, then reluctantly, stood very still. Luke promptly released her.

Holly spun around to face him. "You weren't about to fall back there, were you? You don't seem weak to me," she accused.

"No, I wasn't, but you were too close to the edge just now. You could have lost your balance."

"You led me to believe that you were hurt," she accused again.

"No, that was your idea, Holly. Actually I was looking at the soil just inside the rim. In a safe way, I might add."

"You said you were dizzy...."

"No, you asked if I were dizzy and I said no."

"You said you needed to rest—"

"What I said was that it would be nice to rest for a

52

moment." He looked down at her from his superior height, and though he had a serious expression on his face, his eyes were laughing at her.

Holly knew a moment of uncertainty. She had known Luke Westford less than two days and had been angry with him three times, felt like a fool twice, and she didn't even want to think about the way she had felt back on the path when she had thought he might be in pain. Most of all she didn't want to think about the feelings she had during that brief moment when his arms had held her so close.

She brushed past him on the trail and hurried off in the direction of the car.

"If you feel so great, I'm sure you can make it back to the car by yourself!" Her angry voice floated back up the path to where Luke stood watching her retreating figure.

As Holly ran down the hill toward the car, she tried to concentrate on how angry she was and push from her mind the growing realization of just exactly what it was that was so infinitely disturbing.

It wasn't as if Luke Westford was the first attractive man she had ever met. People came from everywhere to Tannehill and she had never lacked for male attention. It was just that she had never been interested enough to become involved with anyone. She was appalled at the admission of that truth. It wasn't really Luke that was causing the trouble. It was her own awakened heart.

This can't be happening to me, she argued with herself. *I won't fall in love with a man like Luke Westford, a man from another world, a dangerous stormy man who probably collects women as casually as I collect rocks along the bank of Mill Creek.* "I'll only get hurt," she whispered to herself as she thought about his position, wealth, and background. But then she remembered the vivid blue eyes, the strong line of his mouth, and the hardness of his body. Could she resist such a man?

That evening Holly sat in the swing on the porch and thought about the smouldering embers in her heart. As she looked across the circle at a light which was burning in Luke Westford's camper, she hoped desperately that her problem didn't turn into a raging forest fire—out of control.

Chapter Four

But it was too late. The fire was out of control. During the next week and a half, Holly discovered that every time she succeeded in stamping out one portion of the tiny flames that kept springing up inside her, there was another little area ready to take its place and all the while it was spreading. Somehow a forest fire had started in her heart, and Holly didn't know how to stop it.

The time Holly spent with Luke Westford became the most important thing in her life. Her motive of keeping him away from her father slipped into second place, and she had to keep reminding herself of why she had planned such a strategy in the beginning. Any plans for revenge quickly dissipated and were replaced with something more important. She must, at all costs, keep her new feelings locked within. No one, especially Luke Westford, must suspect her secret. She didn't even trust Buddy for fear that he might somehow convey her emotion to Brandy, who would in turn relay it to Luke.

Even if she couldn't stop the flaring sparks of feeling she had for Luke Westford, Holly knew that her sharp remarks were the only weapons she had, the only defense she could use to maintain a barrier between them. She watched a strong bond of friendship grow between her father and Luke, and she reluctantly admitted that Luke Westford would never recommend anything that wasn't in the best interests of everyone concerned, including her father.

So Holly polished up her remaining armor at every opportunity. It was all that she could do since she was obligated to the task of being Luke's guide during his stay at Tannehill.

Something else was at stake, too. Luke's report to the Department of Interior would be a major factor in the government's decision to provide federal money for the expansion of Tannehill. It was also possible that the Regional Commission would be influenced by his opinion.

John Scott seemed to have an extraordinary number of tasks that demanded his attention, and Holly found herself constantly filling in for him as guide and hostess to Luke. Monday afternoon she gave Luke a tour of some of the old buildings located in the park circle.

"Every single piece of the cabins was numbered and marked before they were taken apart. Then the pieces were carefully transported and reassembled according to the numbers," Holly explained as she led the way up the rough plank steps of the Hogan House.

"How many pioneer homes are there at Tannehill?" Luke asked.

"Twenty," Holly answered. At the top step they stopped between the porch posts. "This house dates from 1835. Our dairy barn, built in 1822, is the oldest building in the park."

The wide dogtrot that separated the two main rooms of the house was an extension of the porch. As Holly and Luke walked into the passage, a cool wind blew through the house bearing the faint music of the pines. They peered through iron bars into a dark and musty bedroom. The rough interior and sparce furniture was a far cry from the warm, cheery little cabin that Holly called home.

"This was really roughing it," Luke commented as he looked at the great stone fireplace, the only means of heating, and the rusty lamps that hung from the cabin walls.

Holly glanced at Luke. For some reason it irritated her that he looked so distinguished in jeans and a cotton chambray shirt. She shifted her attention to his hands, which were only inches from hers on the iron bars, hands that were tanned and strong with short clean nails. *Hands that had done a lot of hard work,* she reflected. *Not at all the sort of hands one would expect to see on an Interior Department official.* She spoke to break the spell that Luke had unconsciously cast over her.

"Well, I suppose anyone looking back on an earlier civilization thinks that. Someday people will think that about us, too, even when they're inspecting today's fine homes with double-insulated windows and thick carpets."

Luke looked at her, slim and fragile against the rough walls of the pioneer cabin. There was an indefinable inner strength about her that called to his mind women with that same quality who had survived those early hardships and helped to settle America.

"Well," he said in his best drawl, "you must be the resident philosopher as well as guide."

She cast him a quelling glance. "Don't forget historian," she said. "This was the main house of a small Bibb County plantation." Her tone was sharp and defensive.

"Don't get your fur up, spitfire. I was really giving you a backhanded compliment. Actually, you're not too bad at history or philosophy." Before she could reply, he moved the conversation back to the pioneer buildings. "What about the other homes in the immediate circle?"

"The Thompson House dates from 1835, the Bagley House from 1856, and Marchant, Stewart, and Dunkin houses in the seventies."

"I'd prefer the later cabins, myself," Luke laughed. "These dogtrots must have been rough going during the winters."

"But lovely in summer," Holly said, determined to get the last word.

They crossed the open breezeway and looked into the kitchen; then walked down the steps and out into the sunlight.

"We have time for the bridge and the mill before I have to get supper," Holly said. After an affirmative nod from Luke, they set off down the dusty road.

The bridge was a rare 1902 iron truss relocated from Tapawingo Springs, Jefferson County. Its rectangular canopy was divided into three squares criss-crossed into triangles against the blue of the sky. Luke took particular interest in the bridge and inspected it carefully before jotting some notes into a small pad. Holly watched his well-shaped brown hands write a small neat script and she was struck by the confidence they inspired. Hands like that were capable and responsible.

She was relieved when Luke suggested they walk on toward the mill. For although Holly derived pleasure from his presence, her common sense told her it would be to her advantage when Luke Westford packed up his camper and left Tannehill. The sooner his business was completed, the better for everyone.

The reconstruction of the Hall Grist Mill and Cotton Gin was in progress. Two workmen were assembling the support structure for the mill wheel. After speaking to the men, Holly and Luke explored the mill.

"The mill will grind meal just like it did a century ago," Holly spoke from the shadow of a huge beam.

"When will the mill be in operation?"

"Probably around November."

"You're looking forward to it, aren't you?" Luke asked in response to the slight shadow that had darkened the usual brightness of her voice.

"To the fresh meal, yes. But I don't come down here often. There're so many tales about the mill—some legends, some ghost stories."

Luke looked surprised. "I would have thought that was your cup of tea, Holly."

"Well, I'm not bothered by the ghost stories—it's a real one. A killer-bandit was lynched here in the 1870's."

"Vibrations from the past?"

"I guess so, Luke," she answered, knowing that from now on all the vibrations from the mill wouldn't be bad. She had shared the grist mill with Luke.

The next afternoon Holly found Luke on the porch of the old country store, an 1895 peanut house from Perry County. The store was a chaotic conglomeration of past and present. An assortment of old bottles lined one of the back shelves, a variety of jars another. Charlie had started the collections, and now and then people contributed to the display. His all-time favorite was a green soda bottle complete with metal bottle cap. On the shelf below, various colored cans of soft drinks with pop tops demanded equal attention.

On the adjacent wall, a horse harness darkened with age hung beside a lady's riding crop. Not far from the modern lighting fixture, an old lantern dangled from the ceiling. A huge jar of pickles stood on the counter beside the cash register. Cheerful racks of picture postcards kept company with tin buckets of syrup.

Luke rose from a cane-bottom chair as Holly walked up, his head almost at the level of an old rusty horseshoe that was nailed to the outer wall of the store. As Holly greeted Luke, she was aware of a disapproving glance from Charles, who was opening a large box of potato chips.

"Hi, Holly," Charles mumbled from behind the counter, as he refilled the potato chip rack with the small packages from the box.

"Hi, Charlie," Holly said before she turned her attention to the other man. "I brought a Thermos, Luke." Holly held the green-flowered container up for his inspection. "It isn't all that far to the slave quarters, but a drink of something cool will taste good by the time we get there."

"Holly, can I see you for a minute?" Charles interrupted.

"Sure, Charlie," she said as she walked to the door, sensing correctly that he wished to talk to her privately. Once inside, Charles pulled her into the back of the store.

"Are you going off with him again, Holly?" Charles's brows threatened to collide, wrinkles cascading across his usually unperturbed forehead. "You've been with him almost every day since he's been here. What's your Daddy thinking of, letting you go off with him like that?"

"Daddy isn't letting me, Charlie. He's sending me."

Holly pulled away from his grasp and put her hands on her hips.

He looked at her for a moment as if he didn't believe her. Then in a calmer tone he asked, "You going down to the slave quarters and straight back?"

Holly sidestepped the issue. "If we don't get started, it's going to be dark before we get back." She turned to leave.

"I think I'd better go along and protect you, 'my little turtle dove,' " the inimitable Fields appeared.

"Oh, Charlie," Holly laughed, "I don't need protecting. I'm going to protect him, to be sure he doesn't get off the trail, and to give him information for all those notes he makes."

Without waiting for Charles to argue the point, Holly ran from the rear of the store and out on the porch.

"On the whole," Charlie, alias W. C. Fields, rasped, "I'd rather Westford was in Philadelphia." He grabbed a broom and stirred up dust with quick jabs against the plank floor.

The serene woodland hillside was the burial place of between three hundred fifty to four hundred slaves from the Oglesby Plantation. The sandstone markers had been obliterated by rain, wind, and time.

"Every grave is facing east," Luke commented, looking at the resting places of those who had endured an earthly existence of slavery.

"At least the next time the sun rose they'd be free from slavery. Death was a beginning for them, not an end."

"Were most of the slaves that religious?" Luke asked, looking at the forgotten resting place of men, women, and children.

61

"Some were devout Christians, some just religious, but almost all slaves believed in the Resurrection."

"And you, Holly Scott. Do you believe that story about the Resurrection?"

Her eyes searched his face for a moment. "Yes, Luke, I do."

They looked at each other across the parched dry earth, the essence of yesterday permeating the scene with the sorrows of slavery.

"Do you believe the whole bit," he questioned, "the city of gold and the mansions?"

A smile lifted her mouth. "Things more important than gold and mansions. There will be no tears, pain, crying, or death. Here on earth happiness doesn't come to everyone, but there it will. Sometimes I feel I'm almost there, that Tannehill is a glimpse of Heaven."

At that moment Buddy and Brandy bounded out of the woods into the cemetery, tails juxtaposed in fierce horizontal movement.

"There's a favorite place of mine on the north spur of Shades Mountain. When we get there we'll have some lemonade." Holly led the way, followed by Buddy, Brandy, and Luke.

The four of them dropped to the ground under a black gum tree shaped remarkably like an umbrella. They shared the lemonade in silence as Luke made some notes on the slave quarters.

"Was Tannehill the first owner of the furnace?" Luke asked as he shifted his weight back against a tree and stretched his legs.

"No. Daniel Hillman, Ninian Tannehill, J. B. Green, and Moses Stroup all owned it, but the name Tannehill stuck."

"It's a good name," Luke said. "It goes with this park."

"I think so, too," Holly agreed. "It is a beautiful name."

"Well, Scarlett, it seems we finally agreed on something," Luke teased,

"I wouldn't say that was the first time we ever agreed on anything," Holly argued, not wanting to waste another chance to disagree with him.

He looked at her with a questioning brow.

"Animals," Holly said. "We both feel the same way about them. You use almost the same tone when you're talking to Brandy and Buddy that I do."

At the mention of her name, Brandy moved over close to Holly and flopped down at her side, nudging her hand for a caress, which Holly obligingly bestowed upon her shiny, silky head.

"I dare not agree," Luke said in mock solemn tones. "I've found the easiest way to get along with you is to disagree with whatever you say."

She started to respond to that statement, but changed her mind. "Well, since you're trying so hard to be disagreeable—or rather, agreeable—I'll change the subject." Her own mock crossness dared him to dispute that statement. "Have you had Brandy since she was a pup?"

"No," a shadow fell across Luke's face, a faint veil shading the vivid blue of his eyes. "Brandy belonged to my parents. She was an anniversary present from my father to my mother." He let his hand trail down the sleek fur of the Irish setter, memories of the past passing in review. Then he continued the brief account.

"They were in a wreck a week after that anniversary. My father was killed and my mother confined to a

63

wheelchair for the remaining months of her life. Brandy was unharmed. She was a loving companion in those trying times, first to my mother, then to me."

"Luke, I'm sorry. That's when you transferred to the Midwest, wasn't it?"

Luke nodded, "It isn't painful to me now." Almost as an afterthought, he added, "They shared a lot of good years together, two lifetimes of love."

Holly looked at Luke, unanswered questions in her eyes.

"Do you have brothers or sisters, Luke?" she inquired.

"No, I guess we're alike in one more respect, Holly. I came along late in my parent's life and there were never any more children."

Holly looked at him, absently stroking the setter. Their hands touched and clung, mutual loss gently binding them together.

"How did you get Buddy?" Luke asked.

"Oh,…he came up to the cabin for supper one night, a thin, scraggly, hungry puppy. He just stayed on. We never found who he belonged to. We even advertised in the paper."

"I guess it was your Tannehill stew," Luke joked lightly, but Holly couldn't laugh—not with her hand clasped inside Luke's fingers. "By the way, your father invited me to supper tonight."

"Supper! Daddy has invited you to supper and I haven't even thought about what to fix. It'll be almost dark when we get back."

Luke laughed as he rose and pulled Holly to her feet beside him.

"Buddy may just have to share his Tannehill stew with us tonight, Holly."

Luke ate supper at the Scott cabin frequently in the days ahead, always at John Scott's invitation, for Holly was careful to do nothing that Luke might interpret as her personal interest in him.

One evening before the meal the two men sat and talked on the front porch of the cabin as if they had known each other for years instead of days. From the kitchen Holly heard the muted sounds of their voices and knew she would never hear anything more pleasing. The blending of her father's soft drawl with Luke's vibrant tones was as wonderful as the music of the forest. She never knew how often Luke's eyes strayed to the window to catch a glimpse of her at work in the tiny kitchen.

Holly aimlessly stirred the big pot of soup on the old kitchen stove. Her mind was not on the task, and she slowly raised the long-handled wooden spoon from the pot. She stood at the stove, an apron about her slim waist, with the pot lid raised in her left hand and the big spoon raised in her right while she stared out the window.

Oh, she thought, *it's happened. The two men I love. I love Luke. I love him as much as I love my father—even more, but in an entirely different way.* Her eyes fastened on a beautiful red rose which only that morning had been a bud. *It happened like the roses,* she thought. *The petals just opened so slowly that I didn't even notice and now it's a rose.*

At that moment Luke came into the kitchen. He saw her there, poised and motionless, arms uplifted like a slender doll someone had placed inside a miniature kitchen. The soup bubbled unheeded on the stove.

"You'd better turn down the fire under that pot, Holly," Luke said quietly.

She whirled around, arms still uplifted, eyes wide,

face flushed from her startling discovery. She looked at Luke standing lazily in the doorway, his arms crossed against his chest. The blue of his shirt was no match for the brilliance of his eyes.

Panic raced up Holly's legs and twined about her heart, but it was quickly commuted to anger. Luke had taken her heart without even trying and she had been powerless to stop him. And in a few days he would drive away and take it with him and she couldn't stop that either.

"Are you staying to supper again?" She raised her chin to emphasize the last word.

"I'll be very disappointed if you told me there wasn't enough in that pot for two extras." He surveyed the color of her cheeks and the trance-like expression in her eyes.

"There's plenty for Brandy," she said slowly.

Luke looked at her slender arms still holding the spoon and lid aloft. "What were you thinking about when I disturbed you, Holly?"

"I was looking at the roses. People don't have to think all the time, do they?" She evaded his question without hesitation but the heightened tint of her skin betrayed her.

"Well," Luke drawled in his imitation southern accent, "I suppose if a woman can cook a decent meal and keep house, there's no reason for her to think."

"That's a chauvinistic thing to say," she said sharply.

"About par with your southern hospitality, Holly."

Her father came into the cabin and crossed the front room to his bedroom.

"Luke," she whispered. *It's not his fault that I love him,* she told herself. *He hasn't tried to take my heart and it's wrong of me to blame him for the way I feel.* They stared at each other for a long moment.

"Maybe there isn't enough in the pot tonight, Holly." He said before he crossed the front room and went out the front door.

Holly stood rooted to the floor for a second, then the spoon clattered to the floor. She threw the pot lid on the table and ran after Luke, catching up with him as he reached the ground at the bottom of the front steps.

"Luke, don't go. I didn't mean to be rude. You were right—I *was* thinking about something. I just couldn't share it with you."

He looked down at her stricken face. Suddenly he knew what had happened in the kitchen, as surely as if she had told him. "Things seem to be as stirred up as your soup, Holly. I guess we had both better cool off a little. It's best if I don't stay for supper tonight."

Let him go, her common sense told her, but her heart wouldn't listen.

"But, Luke, Daddy is expecting you to stay."

"Give your father my regrets." He whistled and his faithful Irish setter ripped around the corner of the cabin and heeled on his left.

"Tomorrow, Luke?"

"Tomorrow we'll probably both wonder just what this was all about."

He started across the circle, the setter heeling close. Then he abruptly turned and flashed Holly a disarming smile from the shadows of the pines. "I never cultivated a taste for scorched soup anyway."

"The soup!"

She turned and raced up the steps and into the cabin, his laughter following her. She quickly cut off the flame and surveyed the damage. Soup had boiled over the rim of the pot and formed patches on the stove. A big puddle of soup was in the bottom pan underneath the stove burner. She cautiously put a spoon into the pot. The bottom of the pot was coated with burned food.

Her fighting spirit revived. *Why he knew it was scorching all the time,* she thought. "Luke Westford, tomorrow you may not be able to remember what all the fuss was about, but I will. I will."

Chapter Five

The autumn weather in Birmingham was beautiful. The azure morning sky lightened to a pale hue just above the skyline of the city, while the shadowed sides of tall buildings were a deeper shade of blue that complemented the distant gray mountains. Brilliant fall sunshine reflected from the tinted windows and ricocheted about the city on spikes of light.

On the southern horizon, a magnificent statue of Vulcan stood with his torch stretched to the heavens like an emperor lifting his scepter before loyal subjects.

John Scott had suggested a change of scenery for Luke Westford, commenting that his visit wouldn't be complete without a close-up look at the Magic City. Her father was right, but Holly wondered how much his health had to do with the suggestion. Last night she had noticed the strain on his face as he had quickly dropped into his rocker after Luke left the cabin.

So Holly had accepted her father's proposal that she and Luke drive into Birmingham the next day. And when Luke had suggested that they start early and have breakfast on the way, it seemed so much the better. Perhaps her father would find a few minutes to rest even though his duties were multiplied on Saturdays.

When Holly dressed, she had bypassed her jeans and selected a skirt and blouse. The soft, long-sleeved beige blouse had a shirred front yoke, rounded collar and bow tie. A leather belt banded the waist of her navy, knife-pleated skirt.

Holly had not slept well. Her night had been perforated with restless moments when she relived the discovery that she loved Luke and alternate flashbacks of that exhausted look on her father's face.

The ride into Birmingham had been pleasant but Holly and Luke had little to say to each other, as if neither knew how to pick up the strands after their argument the night before.

"Enjoy your supper last night?" Luke broke into her thoughts as the Catalina pulled into the parking lot of the restaurant Holly had suggested, an inn which hosted a popular Saturday brunch.

"I decided—since you like soup so much—to save it until the next time you eat with us." Holly threw down her gauntlet with a smile.

Luke laughed and the disharmony of the night before dissipated in the sound. He smiled at her broadly as he cut the ignition.

"I should have known you'd think of that. I think I should have stayed for supper last night." He reached for the blue herringbone sport coat lying across the back of the seat between them, pulled it on and then adjusted the cuffs of his shirt. He walked around to Holly's side of the car and opened the door.

"You haven't heard the worst," she threatened, as she put her hand into his. "I decided to starve until today since you're paying for breakfast." She grabbed her shoulder bag with her other hand as he pulled her from the car.

Luke faked a groan. "Then I'm glad I suggested breakfast. I might not have enough money to pay for lunch if you waited that long."

Holly was glad the air had cleared between them. She had been both elated and piqued when her father announced that he and Luke had planned the Birmingham outing without so much as consulting her. Almost as if Luke had read her mind, he responded to the unvoiced thought.

"I was going to talk to you about driving into Birmingham, Holly. That's why I came into the kitchen last night. Your father suggested the trip and I thought about our having breakfast. I don't want you to think we were making plans for your day without asking you."

"Is that an apology?" she asked impudently, his words healing the last vestige of hurt from yesterday's tiff.

"Just explaining," he warned gently, tightening his fingers about hers as they walked toward the entrance to the restaurant. He dropped her hand to catch the brass handle of the enormous carved door, and she turned to him.

"That's good. I don't want to feel guilty about how much I'm going to eat."

Holly made up for Luke's lack of creativity in selecting breakfast. His scrambled eggs, ham, biscuits and potatoes were plain fare compared to her herb omelet surrounded by stuffed mushrooms and bacon rolls.

But the most extraordinary thing about breakfast wasn't Holly's choice of food—it was her new awareness of Luke. She felt as if she had crossed a bridge last night and the toll gate had closed behind her; she had somehow embarked on a journey and having taken the first step, she could not turn back.

They sat at a little table by the window and looked out at the city. In the far distance, Vestavia, the George Ward home designed like a Roman temple, was visible. As they ate, Luke talked about his former job in Washington and shared some tales of college days.

And through it all, her heart refused to listen to reason. She unwillingly admired the strength and sensitivity of his hands. *Get your mind on your mushrooms*, her reason declared. She saw herself in the blue of his eyes as she glanced across the table. *Back to breakfast*, her common sense advised. The waiter broke up the battle as he approached the table and inquired if they would like more coffee.

"Yes," Luke answered for them, "and the lady would like an Alka Seltzer."

The stream of coffee stopped in midair, then resumed. As the rather staid waiter placed the check on the table, his lips twitched a secret smile in Holly's direction. When he was out of hearing range, Holly looked right into Luke's eyes.

"If you say what you're thinking," she stated categorically, "I'm going to order dessert."

"And just what am I thinking?" he asked innocently, deliberately glancing down at her empty plate.

"That you can't believe I ate the whole thing."

Their bantering humor signaled an elusive difference in their relationship. It followed them through the Botanical Gardens, past tall fountains and magnolia trees, around the rose gardens, and under the torii gate to the Japanese teahouse.

At the Museum of Art Holly was more conscious of Luke than of the bronze Remington sculptures of the American west. She found his company more exciting than the Pre-Colombian and South Seas display, his eyes bluer than the Wedgwood collection.

72

From the museum they drove to the spectacular Red Mountain Cut, an engineering feat that carved a road-bed two hundred feet deep and four hundred ten feet wide from the earth. Luke parked the car and they walked out on the elevated walkway that ran a third of a mile down the cut.

The wind shifted, and the gusts intensified through the cut. They stood together in the windswept gap on the side of a sheer cliff towering toward the sky.

Luke interrupted the illusion of their primal isolation as he pointed out a patch reef.

"What makes that odd formation?" Holly asked against the wind.

"Rapid growth of algae plus organisms like corals, sponges and trilobites."

They examined the ore seams and the fault that ran vertically up the cliff, then stood on the ramp and looked at the large pyramid designs cut into the opposite wall of the cut. Below the mountain, a steady stream of cars curved around the expressway.

"It looks as if the cut has meant a lot to Birmingham." Luke turned to face her.

"It's meant a lot of smog drifting out to the hills," she said flatly.

"How can anyone as young as you are be so old-fashioned about progress?"

"Sometimes in the early morning, the smog actually seems to be pouring through the gaps." Her tone was defensive.

That flickering tension between them compounded as his eyes held hers.

"Holly Scott,..." he said slowly, "it just isn't that black and white. There are times when you have to weigh the alternatives to a situation, then make a decision and live with a less than perfect choice.

"I know, Luke," she admitted, "but there's so much gray in the world." The she added with her usual touch of spirit, "I don't have to like it, do I?"

They turned and began the journey back along the walkway.

"No." He smiled. "And if it's any consolation, grey has never been my favorite color."

Vulcan stood boldly on the crest of Red Mountain, his stocky body heavy with muscles from his labor at the forge, his stance befitting the world's tallest cast-metal statue. The colossal iron man, born from the ore of the mountain where he posed, stared impassively out over the city that had created him. The torch he held glowed green against the cloudless day, a sign there had been no traffic deaths.

"I read that several cities had adopted 'light for life' symbols because of Vulcan," Luke said as the car topped Red Mountain and hugged the curve which adjoined Vulcan Park.

"When I was little," Holly reflected, "it always frightened me when we came into Birmingham and the light was red. It still makes me feel a little…"

"Blue?"

"How can you say that with a straight face?" Holly laughed.

Luke slowed the car at the traffic light and turned right. After the steep ascent to the entrance of the park, they pulled into the parking area.

Holly and Luke stopped at the gift shop for coffee, which they carried out under the pavilion to a small, black wrought-iron table. The steaming cups sent spirals of mist into the air. They sat with their backs to the wind blustering across the park. Below, enormous goldfish in an oval pond flicked amber tails and darted here and there in search of bits of food.

"Speaking of memories, I remember thinking when we read all those Roman myths in grade school that you know you're ugly when your mother takes one look at you and throws you off Mt. Olympus." Luke looked across the table at Holly, his eyes following the classical beauty of her face as she gazed at the hills.

Her eyes came back to his. "There's a picture of Vulcan I especially like in a book at home. He's hammering out thunderbolts for Jupiter over a volcano."

"Mine was a picture of the maidens he made from pure gold." Luke mentally compared the images of his youth with the beauty of the woman across the table. Not one of the Vulcan's maidens, he admitted, was as pure or as lovely. With that thought, he collected the cups and deposited them in a container.

The octagon base of the statue was bordered by a concrete walk. As they slowly circled the structure, Luke surveyed the muscular derriére of the god of the forge.

"Vulcan has been a source of pride for Birmingham...and of some contention," Holly remarked. "Most of it about his bare bottom."

"He is a...powerful figure." Luke warily tested his words.

"The people on this side feel...I was going to say slighted, but that's not exactly the right phrase...more like offended. Everybody likes the Iron Man but wants his backside to face somebody else."

"How long has this been going on?"

"Well, his lack of modesty has been discussed off and on for years, but we didn't have this particular problem when he was put up because this side of the city was not very developed. Now it's an affluent residential area."

A gust of wind greeted them as they rounded the northeast angle of the walk.

"One solution," Holly continued, "is to give him a pair of designer jeans or overalls."

"I think I've heard everything," Luke said dryly.

"Not quite," Holly countered. "You haven't heard my solution."

"Something tells me I don't want to hear it."

"A revolving pedestal. He could turn around and around and please everybody."

"Or displease everybody. And I don't suppose cost ever crossed your mind? You're suggesting putting a statue a third of the size of the Statue of Liberty on a revolving pedestal?" Luke opened the door of the exhibition museum in the base of the tower supporting Vulcan, and stood aside for Holly.

"We're not discussing cost," she argued, "just solutions."

Inside, displays told the history of the statue—how Giuseppe Moretti sculpted his dream in an eight-foot high model, of the nineteen million people who viewed Vulcan at the St. Louis World's Fair, about the years he lay disassembled and deserted at the Birmingham Fairgrounds, and finally, of his journey to a home on the mountain.

The center of the circular area was sealed off, the door ajar. Holly pulled the door open to reveal the stairs to the top.

Inside the circular staircase a sense of closeness crowded in on them. The stark white marble walls and stairs added to the sense of claustrophobia.

"We had to walk up before the elevator was installed," Holly recalled.

"Don't tell me. You like the stairs better."

"That's a pretty good guess, Luke. Want to climb up?"

"Do you think you can climb anything after all that breakfast?"

"Oh, yes, I'm working up an appetite for lunch now." Not waiting for him to agree, she ran up the first two flights.

Luke took the steps two at a time, catching up to her at the third landing.

"That's not fair." Holly said noting the ease with which he took the steps in twos.

"You should have thought of that." He moved ahead of her.

The white marble gave way to rough walls plastered with vivid graffiti—dates—vows—lovers.

Several flights up, Luke realized Holly had stopped on the landing below him. He turned and looked down at her.

"Too much breakfast?" he asked smoothly.

"No, I'm looking for my name." Holly searched the writing on the wall. "I wrote it here years ago. I remember which section because it was my birthday and I counted a flight for each year."

He walked back down the stairs and helped her hunt for the lost name, but the childhood autograph was not to be found.

"Got a pencil?" he asked, and when Holly produced one from the bottom of her purse, he began to write an H in a vacant spot in the corner. The pencil point was almost worn away when he completed the letter.

"I don't have another pencil." Holly began to scratch in her purse for something else to write with.

"This is enough," he said, drawing a horizontal line from the bottom of the second bar of the H to make an L.

"Very clever." Holly looked at their joined initials. "Where did you study art?" Her question covered the strange sensation she felt at the thought of their names linked together there on the wall.

"From my Mother Goose Coloring Book," he said levelly, as they continued the long climb.

Before they reached the observation deck, breakfast did take its toll. Holly slowed down, and Luke reached the top before her. But he turned, stepped down a couple of steps, and held out his hand to her. She considered refusing his help, then extended her hand. He pulled her to the top of the stairs in one strong movement.

Luke drew her close as she came to his level, and Holly felt the magnetism in that half embrace. His eyes searched the uncertainty of hers, and his hands discerned the slight tremble of her fingers. He released her and they walked out into the tower.

The view was breathtaking. The city sprawled across Jones Valley, a collage of blue and gray. A single railroad junction had grown into an industrial giant, open mines and the company store replaced by offices, parks, and factories.

They looked at the patriotic memorabilia on the walls, and turned for a last look at the striking view of the valley before they took the glass elevator down.

On the ground terrace, a fierce wind surged from the mountains, molding Holly's skirt to her slender figure and tugging at her hair. Through the eye of the telescope mounted on a platform, they pinpointed the threads that wove the fabric of the city: a poodle wearing a red vest, the monotonous balconies of an apartment complex, a home half hidden on a cliff.

The walk led around a small formal garden to Prayer Point. They stood silently, fingers almost touching on the concrete guard wall, and looked at the city.

Their banter was gone, and in its place a thoughtful quietness. Luke turned and leaned against the wall, his brilliant gaze unfathomable. Holly wondered if he, too, was aware of the new dimension in their relationship.

The fury of the wind increased, hurling Holly's golden hair about her face. She pulled a scarf from her purse and tried to secure her hair, but the blasts thwarted her attempts. Luke caught the scrap of silk and slipped it into his pocket.

"Leave your hair loose, Holly—free, like your spirit."

Holly turned her back to the turbulence as Luke stepped back to read the bronze plaque on the railing of Prayer Point. In that interval, her reason lost the battle of the day. Her eyes noted the sculptured cut of his mouth, the way his coat was slung across his arm and the white shirt stretched across his shoulders, the way his hair tapered to his collar.

There were three scriptures on the plaque. Luke silently read the first two, but he read the third aloud, his voice beckoning her from her reverie. "Surely the Lord is in this place."

Holly chose a famous Chinese restaurant in the heart of the city for a very late lunch, or as Luke insisted, an early dinner. A willowy Amerasian hostess led them to a private curtained dining room. Her exquisite traditional gown hugged her unusually tall figure, and her equally exquisite dark eyes lingered on Luke's face after she handed them menus.

As the woman turned to leave, Holly looked at the long black hair caught into an intricate design at the back of her head. Then she remembered that her own hair was still windblown in spite of a brushing and that her face was flushed from the wind. She felt like a mannequin in a small town store window competing with a model from Vogue.

They enjoyed the sweet hot tea and fragrant chow mein, and their talk drifted from the superb food to the stone and iron sculptures of the Japanese tea garden they had visited earlier in the day and back to food again.

Ceremoniously, they inspected the fortune cookies they had selected from the basket brought by the waiter. Impulsively, Holly reached across the table and touched Luke's hand. He looked at her, the intense blue gaze causing her to withdraw her fingers.

"Let's trade," she suggested lightly, offering him hers.

"You want my fortune?" he asked in pretentious disbelief.

"It might make things...interesting."

"I'm not sure it's a good idea. What if mine says I'm going to receive a million dollars?"

"What if mine does?"

"You're tempting fate," he argued, refusing to relinquish his treasure.

"I don't believe in fate." Holly held the fortune cookie in the palm of her open hand.

"What do you believe, Holly?" Luke asked softly, folding her fingers about the confection and enclosing her small hand in his.

"Our destiny doesn't include fate, Luke."

"A divine map?"

"Yes."

"And if you don't read the road signs?"

"Then you detour. It's like singing off-key. But you

can find the way if you listen for directions, if you can hear the melody."

It was a sentient spell, her hand in his across the table, behind them a tapestry of golden dragons and pagodas, and in the corner, a graceful urn of pink silk cherry blossoms.

"Like taking your cue from the choir director?" he asked half joking, half serious.

"Yes." Holly smiled. "He cues us in. But we do the singing. We make the music."

There was a poignant silence. Then he thoughtfully and slowly unfolded her fingers, and replaced the crescent cookie she held with his.

Holly broke it, and read the message. She raised the back of her hand to her forehead in a gesture of theatrical horror.

"Oh, no! I got your fortune!"

He reached over and took the little paper from her. He read it without even a hint of a smile. "Beware of tall dark strangers."

"So you did." He solemnly agreed.

At that second the beautiful willowy hostess came through the curtains to their table and fastened her dark eyes on Luke. She asked if they desired anything else and Luke told her how delicious the meal had been while Holly kept her eyes on the tea in the bottom of her cup.

After the woman left, Holly giggled, relieved that the laughter she had suppressed could finally be released.

"Are you psychic?" Luke cracked his cookie and read the message.

"No" she said waiting for him to share his fortune. "What does it say?"

"Let's just say that I got your fortune." A cryptic smile slashed his face as he picked up the message and slipped it into his pocket with Holly's scarf.

"Luke," she demanded, exasperation in her voice, "did you get my million?"

He pulled out her chair and they walked across the restaurant and out the door to the music of the wind chimes.

"Luke—" Holly insisted, only to be interrupted.

"I think we'd better head back to Tannehill before you get hungry again."

"I'll trade you, Luke. Dinner tomorrow for my fortune."

"Now it's your fortune?"

"Yes. I got yours."

He hesitated, then inquired suspiciously, "Are you having soup?"

It was her turn to think it over. "All right, no soup, but you'll have to dry the dishes."

"You strike a hard bargain, woman." Luke pulled the scrap of paper from his pocket and handed it to her.

Holly read, then reread the message. She slowly repeated it aloud. "Beware of tall dark strangers." She folded it into a little accordion, tilted her chin high and looked at him. "I think I've been ripped off."

"Sorry, Scarlett." Luke took her hand as they walked toward the parking lot. "A bargain's a bargain."

The Magic City ushered in evening. A crazy quilt of lights emerged in the dusk, streetlamps spotlighting the yellow chrysanthemum blossoms which filled the green dividing Twentieth Street.

As the Catalina pulled up the ramp to the freeway, Holly glanced into the side mirror. The dying sun had left a legacy of maroon and wine. And, as if to remind her of the imminent danger of losing her heart to a tall dark stranger, crimson flowed from Vulcan's torch.

Chapter Six

Luke and Holly stood on the tramway above Furnace No. 1, looking out over Roupe's Creek. Upstream, tourists were already enjoying the spring-fed waters in the popular swimming hole.

Holly had not talked much to Luke since their trip into Birmingham. John Scott had asked his help in securing funds for the expansion of Tannehill, and every afternoon during the past week Holly had found them working over a growing stack of papers on the living room table. *At least,* Holly had thought, *Daddy is sitting and not walking so much.*

"In time Tannehill will probably develop a legend about its beginning." Luke looked at the slight figure of the girl beside him. He never tired of her compelling beauty and innocence.

"It might be like 'Colter's Hell.' " Holly pointed out. "All parks don't have legends about their beginnings."

"Have you been reading up on parks?" he teased.

"No, but I know about Yellowstone," she replied.

"Then you know the Indians regarded it as a place where evil spirits dwelled."

"Well, how about moving the mountain people out of Shenandoah? Forcing four hundred families to move from their homes isn't exactly my idea of an interesting legend."

"Most of those families were willing to move."

"How about the ones who weren't?"

Luke looked at her thoughtfully. "Talking with you is like playing monopoly, Holly. We always end up back at square one." He took a pen from his shirt pocket and turned to look at the tramway.

"Would two hundred dollars buy my way out of jail?" Holly asked softly. Then she added, "But it's not square one—it's GO."

"Will you throw in a railroad?" Luke laughed. "And it's not jail—it's doghouse."

"I'll even throw in Park Place if you'll tell me what it's like to go to Mesa Verde or Carlsbad." She looked up at him, returning his smile.

"It's difficult to describe the cliff dwellings at Mesa Verde, or the Rock of Ages at Carlsbad, or what it's like to ride the High Sierra Trail." He looked out over the mountains as he spoke, the panoramic memories emerging against the gold-tipped trees and smoky mountains.

Holly knew from his voice that the places he mentioned were a vital part of Luke's life and she felt closer to him because of it.

"You've been a lot of places, haven't you, Luke?"

"I suppose so."

"And met lots of different people."

"Yes, but that's not so important, either, Holly, as just who it is you've known."

She silently agreed with him, knowing that he was becoming more important than Charlie or any other boy she had ever dated and that he had changed her life more than all of them together.

"Tell me about some of those legends you were talking about earlier." Her eyes revealed her genuine interest in the subject.

"The kind that generally evolve in our country are Indian lore, folklore or mountain stories."

"How about a particular legend about one of the parks?"

"Some of our parks get their names from legends, like the Wind Cave National Park. The Sioux believed the four winds were gods and the wind was the breath of life. This particular cave was the sacred place from which all the buffalo came. They were sent forth from the cave by the Great Mystery, Wokan Tanka."

"I guess that's why they fought so desperately to keep the Black Hills," Holly said, wondering why her history classes at the university were never this interesting.

"There are hundreds of chambers in the Wind Cave, some a hundred feet high, but the only natural opening was a hole about eight by twelve inches. The wind rushed in and out that little opening."

"Nothing comes cheap, does it, Luke? Everything that's beautiful or grand has such a price tag on it."

Luke glanced down at her. He knew he was glimpsing the real Holly—a young woman who was profoundly affected by the sorrows of others, by the helpless wounded creatures of the forest, and by the underdogs of the past. Finally, he said, "We've got a lot of notes to make so we had better get on with it."

He made copious notes on the furnace, the foundry, the cast and forge house and the blower house, and then shorter entries on the dam, raceway, and run-off ditch. Afterwards he stood, dwarfed by the size of the furnaces, and examined the rich earth that had lured men to plunder for hidden treasure and seek their fortune from the bosom of the hills. He looked at all that was left of man's struggle against nature—dark silent monoliths.

"Sorry you Yankees destroyed it?"

Holly, my brave one, he thought. *You've faced your problem squarely, haven't you. Then you've girded yourself with that prickly little armor of words.* He looked at the defiant tilted chin. "Are you sorry your southern vandals helped finish off the job?"

Holly turned away without answering. The furnaces made Luke think of the fortress Holly had built around herself since he had been there. *Would it crumble at my touch,* he wondered, then put the thought from him, as if he had no right to think that.

As they walked back toward the main circle, they paused to watch the ducks paddle upstream, then float back with the current of Roupe's Creek. Some paraded solid white feathers, others flicked brown-speckled wings, wiggled black-satin-tipped tails, or puffed up brown chests. They looked at the man and the young woman with a questioning turn of sleek green heads.

Holly and Luke took the left fork of the trail. After a short distance and a steep climb up a rugged hill, they found themselves at the ridge, which overlooked the quarry.

"The ironmaster stood right here and bossed the cutting of the sandstone rocks used to build the furnace," Holly commented, pausing beside a large split rock.

"How much do these things weigh?" Luke asked, running his hand over the small indentures where dry oak pegs had been pounded into the sandstone, then soaked to split the huge rocks.

"Not much," Holly bantered, "about five hundred pounds each."

"I say that's enough," Luke said dryly. "It makes me

think of building a pyramid."

"I say it was a tough way to make a living." Holly had the last word as she led the way down from the ridge.

Just as the trail leveled out, a young deer unexpectedly appeared in the path. Soft dark eyes stared at them for a moment, then, as if the animal had made a momentous decision, he walked closer.

"Hello, Kingpin," Holly said, holding out her hand toward the young buck.

Luke watched the encounter from about three feet away.

"Don't let Kingpin fake you off, Luke," Holly laughed. "He's a genius at getting treats. He makes you think you're the first person he's ever approached if you're out here on the trail."

Alert ears twiched as Kingpin nuzzled the palm of Holly's hand with his beautiful nose. Disappointed, he turned to look at Luke.

"I'd almost swear he's smiling," Luke laughed as he joined the pair. Immediately the deer tried to entice a treat from Luke.

"We didn't bring any food with us, Kingpin," Holly sighed regretfully. She watched Luke softly stroking the deer under his chin. Kingpin moved his head back as if he were crowned with eight points instead of three-inch spikes.

"There's one predictable thing about Kingpin," Holly declared jokingly. "You can never tell when he's going to pop up. Sometimes he picks very inopportune moments. He thinks he owns this park."

"So that's where he got his name." When Holly nodded, Luke added, "He's a ham actor, too."

"You should see him down in the circle. He's better than my rendition of Scarlett."

Kingpin bounded away as quickly as he had appeared, on his way in search of unsuspecting hikers, hopefully with pockets full of treats.

When Luke and Holly reached the cabin, John Scott was in his favorite rocker on the porch. After they had exchanged greetings, John insisted that Luke stay for lunch and then informed Holly not to make any plans for Sunday afternoon.

"I'd like for you to go with Luke down to Sadler House." John Scott puffed leisurely on his pipe, sending aromatic spirals to the rafters.

And Holly, who knew she should make up some excuse not to be with Luke so much, lost a quick argument with her heart and went on feet of wings into the kitchen to prepare their food.

Sadler House, a two-story, dogtrot-style plantation house built before 1840, was shadowed by a towering shade tree, its lower rectangular structure topped by a smaller long thin second floor. Twin chimneys stood like honor guards on either end of the house.

The dogtrot was cool and dark and the wind that blew through the porch reminded Holly of the legend Luke had told her of the Wind Cave. She had worn a dress as a concession to her father, and the flared skirt moved easily about her knees. The scoop neck and sleeveless bodice of pale green linen made Holly a vision of coolness in the autumn heat.

Sadler House was a mixture of the sounds, scents, and shadows of history, a powerful stimulus to Holly's overactive imagination. As she and Luke walked through the old house, she blinked at a shadow that caught her peripheral vision.

"What is it, Holly?" Luke asked as he examined the rough texture of the walls.

She didn't answer for a moment—it would sound so absurd.

"I thought I saw a gingerbread man dancing in the firelight," she whispered. "And there isn't even a fire in the fireplace."

Luke glanced at the cold dark recess in the wall. "You mean the one with the white icing hat and striped candy cane?"

"Oh, Luke!" She laughed and gave him a special smile. Then she closed her eyes and enjoyed the fragrances of the past that wafted through the room. "Can't you smell the peppers and onions hanging from the rafters and popcorn exploding over the fire and beaten biscuits and hot wassail—"

"Hot wassail?" Luke interjected and raised his brows in doubt.

"It really is a Christmas favorite in these parts."

"And what else do you see, Holly?"

"Flickering candlelight...and I can hear dulcimer music drifting through the window."

"And children's laughter?" Luke added, remembering that he had been an only child, a fact that had been a source of regret to himself as well as his parents.

"Yes, especially children's laughter."

They went back out into the beautiful afternoon, the sun warm on them after the coolness of the house. They stopped beside the car and looked back at Sadler House, a rustic nostalgic scene under a cloudless canopy of blue.

"Shall we take the long way home, Holly?"

"Yes, it's a lovely day for a drive, and there are no night services at church on Sundays or Wednesdays," she agreed.

An hour later, Luke stopped the car at the Mud Creek bridge.

"The Furnace Master's Inn will be built there this time next year." Holly looked to her right. "It will have two dining levels and a big porch with rockers so you can rest after you've eaten too much ham and black-eyed peas." Her eyes twinkled at the thought of the porch lined with guests too full to walk.

"Another revival of southern soul food?"

"Ham and black-eyed peas have never been out of style here, Luke. It just so happens we're having that for supper tonight."

"Was that an underhanded invitation?"

"Well,…" she deliberately hesitated. Then she added firmly. "Yes, it certainly was."

"Well,…" he mocked her hesitation, "it's about time."

"Time for what?"

"That *you* invited me to supper, Holly."

The evening meal was delicious. A large oval bowl of black-eyed peas, generous slices of fried center-cut ham, and thick wedges of golden cornbread filled with butter graced the table. John Scott ate his last piece of buttered cornbread with sorghum, and though Luke declined that finishing sweet touch, he watched in appreciation as John enjoyed his.

Holly declined Luke's offer to help with the dishes. "You both look as if you need to sit in the front porch rockers," she said mischievously. "I'll bring out some coffee in a few minutes to revive you." As the men left the kitchen, she filled the dog bowls with crunchy chunks of dog meal and Tannehill ham stew.

She cleared the table, stacked the dishes in the sink and covered them with a flowered tea towel. Buddy woofed to go outside and Brandy cleaned her bowl and followed him out the back door of the cabin.

When Holly carried the two mugs of fresh coffee to the front porch, she found her father and Luke deep in conversation about the expansion of the park. She quietly left the coffee and returned to the kitchen.

Luke appeared in the doorway just as she had swept the last crumbs out the door and hooked the screen. He looked at the dishes neatly stacked and covered with the colorful towel.

"That was fast," he commented.

Holly smiled, thinking that she had learned something useful in high school after all—her favorite teacher had taught her that trick. The dishes were still dirty.

A deep rumble from the mountains echoed through the valley.

"I knew it was too beautiful to last," Holly said with regret.

"We had better whistle up the dogs," Luke stepped out the back door.

The roses tossed red and yellow heads in the wind that had sprung up, and fallen leaves scurried across the upper trail.

Luke whistled, waited a few moments, then whistled again.

"I hope they haven't gone far," Holly frowned as she walked back through the house to the front porch. Luke joined her and they stood together watching the increasing velocity of the wind. The tall pines swayed like giant broom-straws.

"We'd better see if we can find them, Luke."

"Your father walked down to the store, Holly. Maybe they followed him."

Before they reached the store, they were met by John Scott.

"Brandy and Buddy crossed over the creek," John

said, pointing in the direction of the Garden of Inspiration. "You two better call them in and hurry on back before the storm breaks."

They ran across the bridge and past the Marchant House. Luke whistled again but there was no response.

A jagged bolt electrified the sky, illuminating a vast formation of boiling, rolling clouds. Darkness fell over the valley, the last moments of afternoon sun blotted from the earth.

"Holly, we've got to go back. This is going to be a bad one."

"Oh, Luke, Buddy is terrified of storms. He's just a big baby when it comes to thunder and lightning."

"Brandy isn't. They'll find a shelter and we've got to find one ourselves."

Rain hit the dusty earth, first with big soft drops, then with such force that the drops seemed to bounce up knee high. The pines danced, unwilling participants in a frenzied ritual, wielding great arms of green.

They ran back toward the cabin, but as they passed the barbecue pavilion, Luke pulled Holly into the shelter.

"We've lost Brandy and Buddy," she uttered a cry of dismay and started out into the storm again, all danger to herself forgotten.

Luke's arms went about her, pulling her back from the lashing rain, his chest a refuge from the whipping wind.

"I've got to find them," her voice was lost in the howls of the storm as she tried to free herself from his hold.

"Buddy and Brandy are safe, Holly. I just saw your father let them into the cabin."

Luke gathered Holly into his arms and carried her to the huge stone fireplace at the end of the shelter. He held her in his arms as they sat close to the stones, the center of the projection a partial umbrella against the stinging rain.

A wild melody resounded through the woods. The pines arched and bowed their backs, threatening the earth with sweeping green plumes.

"We'll just have to wait it out here, Holly," Luke spoke against the damp curls.

"Daddy must be frantic," she whispered.

"He saw us take shelter. It's as safe here as in your cabin." He heard a little sigh of relief and felt her relax against him. Luke pulled her closer into the circle of his arms.

Holly wasn't afraid of the storm. She had implicit faith and had never seen a storm she wasn't certain that the Creator of the winds and seas controlled. She didn't tell Luke she wasn't afraid. This moment was nothing to him and it was everything to her.

In the midst of a great storm she was experiencing the thing she had longed for most since she had met Luke. She was in his arms, her face pressed against his heart, her hands warmed by the muscles of his back.

Night fell on Tannehill and the grey curtain of rain cut Holly and Luke off from the rest of the world.

Tomorrow, Holly thought, *Luke won't even remember this moment while I will cherish it forever.*

Chapter Seven

The third weekend in October ushered in the first crisp air of winter. The cool wind from the mountains tumbled over Tannehill and spread out in the valley like fog rolling in from the sea.

Ordinarily, Holly would have savored the beauty of the turning leaves—the deep scarlet dogwoods bearing bright red fruits, the sassafras flaunting mitten-shaped flags, and maples wearing coats of many colors—but this year each day of unfolding beauty brought Luke closer to leaving. Each drifting leaf that floated down to carpet the forest floor brought her one moment closer to the morning she would walk out of her cabin and look across Tannehill to the vacant spot where Luke's camper had been parked.

October's third weekend also heralded Trade Day, a tradition at Tannehill. The park had begun to fill Friday morning and by nightfall almost every spot had been taken. By Saturday morning four thousand people were jammed into the park, trading and buying arts, crafts, and flea market items.

In the distance Holly could hear a group of folk musicians playing a spirited familiar tune. But she had no joy in the early morning music or the approaching day.

To Holly, it was just a necessary interruption of the peace and serenity of the park. She looked in the direction of Luke's camper a dozen times that morning but saw nothing of him. Finally, after lunch, with her swimsuit on under her jeans and shirt, she whistled for Buddy and ran up the hill in back of the cabin.

They roamed the woods while sunlight poured into the valley and penetrated through the trees, warming the land and coaxing it into a beautiful Indian Summer day. An hour later they stopped at their favorite secluded glen in Roupe's Creek.

The chatoyant artistry of the stream was enchanting. The water reflected the myriad greens of the woodlands and turned silver as it brushed the rocks. Trees stretched golden branches over the stream to form a temple of nature.

"This might be our last chance to swim this year, Buddy," Holly's voice was muffled by the shirt she was stripping over her head.

Buddy needed no more encouragement. He was in the water before she had slipped her jeans off. Holly waded into the water slowly, securing her hair atop her head with ribbon and pins. Her figure, though slight, was perfectly formed, slender legs tapering from gently rounded hips to small arched feet. She took a deep breath and sank into the water, gliding out across the creek.

As she turned and started back, she saw Luke leaning against a pine tree. She was too startled to speak and she was grateful that Brandy began to bark at Buddy. She looked at the Irish setter for a moment trying to gather her wits.

"What are you two doing here?" She treaded water as she spoke in what she hoped was a casual tone.

"Looking for you."

Those three words made the day unreasonably brighter, but she couldn't think of an immediate response. She switched the conversation to a safer topic.

"I thought you'd be at Trade Day."

"I knew you wouldn't be there, so when I didn't find you at home, I let Brandy have a try at finding Buddy."

Luke shifted from his stance against the tree and walked to the edge of the water. Brandy ran around his legs twice and circled back to Buddy.

"How's the water?" he asked from his vantage point on a tree trunk that jutted out over the creek.

"Cold, but there won't be many days left to swim this year. Any day now winter will move in to stay." She continued to tread water, wishing she had listened to her father and bought a bathing suit with a little more to it.

"You're right." Luke looked up at the brilliant autumn sunlight filtering through the trees, making a collage of green and gold along the creek bank and dappling the water with gold dust.

"Too bad you didn't bring your suit," Holly said, secretly glad that she didn't have to share the intimacy of swimming with him.

"As a matter of fact, I did," Luke laughed as he peeled the blue knit shirt over his head and slung it over a limb. His lean muscular chest was the same bronzed teak as his arms; wide shoulders slimmed to a narrow waist. "Your father told me you had gone swimming."

At that moment Brandy joined Buddy and the two dogs converged on Holly, barking and paddling in a friendly chase. In the midst of the excitement, Luke surfaced behind Holly and skimmed water at her. After a short, one-sided water battle, Holly retreated and swam downstream, her usually smooth crawl hampered by a strange nervousness that she knew was related to Luke's proximity. Luke caught up with her easily, his powerful arms and legs cutting the water.

They swam until the stream widened and Holly's toes touched the bottom. The water was chest high on Holly, but it barely reached Luke's waist.

"Let's rest a while," Luke motioned to a large flat rock on the bank that looked smooth and sun-warmed.

Black willows with irregular spreading branches dangled thin, narrow leaves above the creek. Brilliant red blackgums and graceful scarlet sourwoods swayed in the background, thin pencils of light making flames of their crimson leaves.

"It would be nice to rest a little," agreed Holly, aware that her breathlessness had little to do with swimming.

They waded ashore, Luke's longer strides enabling him to reach the rock first. He reached out to pull her up on the rock. Her free hand held to his arm for support, encountering a corded wetness that reminded her of the steel that had been forged and cooled in the creek.

Luke released her fingers and sat down on the rock. Holly dropped down beside him, wrapping her arms about her knees for warmth. The sun dried their skin and took the chill from their bodies. Luke stretched out and relaxed, hands folded behind his head for a pillow. After a few minutes, Holly followed suit.

Buddy and Brandy came ashore, and after much shaking, settled down together on a nearby bed of pine straw.

Holly looked up at the startling beauty of the forest with its unsurpassed palette of colors. She knew the woods·had never been so beautiful and that being with Luke had made it that way. The scents of the forest drifted through the air, and the sound of the creek tumbling over the rocks was like the music of a harp. Above the sanctuary of the glen, the sky was a flawless azure marquee.

Neither of them spoke. The silence wasn't awkward—it was sweeter than words. Holly knew then there was no place she had rather be, and more important, no person she would rather be with than Luke.

As for Luke, this afternoon had made clearer to him what he had known from the beginning—he loved Holly.

He had loved her from that first day and his love had grown until she had filled his heart and life. He smiled to himself. Strange that love should come to him now, after he had decided that it was only a dream that eluded men. Strange that after all these years a young woman of the woods had stolen his heart and she hadn't even been trying. He remembered some of the sophisticated women in his past. Each one had seemed to leave his heart a little colder than before.

Luke hadn't meant to love Holly.

She's too young, he thought. *Too innocent. Holly, with her kind gentle ways and unpretentious attitude toward life. Holly, a woodland nymph who loves the forest and animals as much as I do. Holly, who doesn't know how beautiful she is or how her loveliness stirs my heart.*

He didn't know whether the music that he heard was made by the pines or was in his mind.

"Holly," he said softly, turning over on his side and propping up on his elbow, "do you hear that music?"

"Yes, Luke," a silver ribbon of laughter threaded through her voice. Her eyes were closed and her hair, dried to golden tendrils, curled against the darkness of the rock. She opened her eyes and almost wished she hadn't, for the vivid blue of Luke's eyes was so close to hers.

"It's the singing of the pines and the murmur of the creek mixed with the...cadence of your heart." She whispered so the tempo of the music wouldn't change. "Not everyone can hear it, Luke. It's the song of Tannehill." She couldn't look away from the blue of his eyes.

Luke had to use all the self-restraint he possessed at that moment. He wanted to hold her close, to taste the sweetness of her lips, to kiss her eyes closed again. He considered the consequences because he knew it wouldn't be a casual kiss.

He lay back against the rock and looked up at the sky, trying to shut her tantalizing beauty from his mind.

"Do you hear it often, Holly?"

"The music is always there, Luke. It's just that you have to stop and listen before you can hear it. And you have to want to hear it."

"I see," he said slowly, rolling over on his stomach. He reached out and touched a strand of her hair. It felt like fine silk between his fingers.

"Sometimes the music is sad, when the song is from the past—of the days when the slaves labored and died here."

"And other times?"

"Sometimes it's joyous and happy. Once I heard it sound like a great pipe organ, filling the mountains with a great anthem." Her eyes were innocent and childlike as she told him of the woodland concertos. "Then again," her voice trailed off, "it's almost like a lullaby...."

"And, today, Holly?"

"Today, Luke?" she whispered.

"What do you hear today, Holly?"

Today it's a love song, Luke, she thought immediately, but she couldn't say that, so instead she said, "It's not any of those today. It's a different song."

She looked straight into his eyes, not daring to look away lest he guess what she had heard. But as she looked into that blue intensity, she had the strangest feeling he knew exactly what she had heard.

What she couldn't see was Luke's fingers tightening on the silky strand of her hair.

"Perhaps it's a ballet for fairies and elves," Luke laughed down at her, breaking the awesome spell that threatened to cut off her breathing.

They laughed together as shadows fell across the creek, the brilliant colors dulled by twilight, the golds burnished to amber, the flame leaves toned to quiet embers, and the greens hushed to deep emerald.

Long shadows touched them with cool fingers and Holly shivered, once again aware of her damp swimsuit.

"We'd better head for home." Luke rose to his feet and reached out his hand to Holly who unhesitantly put her fingers into his. The evening wind blew her hair across her face, and as Luke tucked the offending strand back into place, his strong, work-worn hands touched her cheek. His eyes softened and seemed to envelop Holly in a warm mysterious web that threatened to draw her against him.

Luke started to say something, but instead turned her unresisting fingers in his firm grasp and led her up the creek bank to where they had left their clothes.

Walking back toward the center of the park, her

hand entwined in Luke's, Holly wished there was no tomorrow—just today.

When they reached the top of the ridge behind the Scott cabin, they paused and looked down at the throngs milling in the park circle. She hated to leave the serenity of the woods, and she hated to leave Luke even more. But there was no way to stop the passage of time and it was only a step away to the spot where their paths would separate. Luke and Brandy would follow the bank of the creek back to their camper, while she and Buddy had to stay close to the woods until the back of their cabin was in sight.

She disengaged her fingers from his. She could not cling to him. She would not cling to him. For in the end she would have to let him go.

Luke reached down and snapped on Brandy's leash, then he straightened up and looked at Holly.

"I have to go to Russell Cave tomorrow, Holly, but I'll be back on Friday. Will you reserve the same campsite for me?"

"Yes," she said, trying not to let the disappointment show, trying to stifle the awful feeling that was clutching at her heart. Her mind clung to his last words. At least he was coming back.

"We could keep Brandy for you, Luke. Then you wouldn't need to move the camper."

"That would be a real favor, if you're sure you don't mind."

"It wouldn't be any trouble. She can stay with Buddy and Daddy until I get home in the afternoons."

"I'll bring her over tomorrow. You check with your father and make sure it's all right with him."

"You don't need to worry about that, Luke." There was nothing left to say, no way to prolong the parting. "Have a good trip, Luke." She turned to leave.

"Holly, some friends of mine will be in Birmingham next weekend. Would you drive in with me for dinner Saturday?"

The band about her heart began to loosen. "Yes."

A smile tugged at the corners of his mouth at her rapid agreement. "We're supposed to meet at Victoria Station at seven. How long will it take us to get there?"

"About an hour."

"Then I'll be over a little before six."

"Don't leave Brandy in the camper. Bring her to the cabin."

"See you Friday, Holly." He inclined his head and smiled down at her. For a fleeting moment a memory he had stored of her flashed through his mind. She looked exactly as she had that first afternoon he had arrived at Tannehill—damp jeans and shirt, hair which had dried to golden tendrils in the sun, eyes that would haunt him as much tomorrow as yesterday.

"Take care, Luke," she said as she returned his smile and turned down the path toward the cabin.

She longed to turn and look back but her pride wouldn't let her. Luke was a strong man and she would not let him see her weakness. She resolved inwardly to keep it that way between them. He wasn't hers; she would make no claim on him.

As she and Buddy ran down the path, she made another resolution. She would not think of the lonely days between now and Friday. She would think only of the moments they had shared together. She would not think of the day when he would leave Tannehill forever. She would think of today and hear again the music they had shared by the creek.

Then, as if in answer to her heart, a soft wind stirred through the hills and drew a bow across the pines, once again filling the valley with the song of Tannehill.

Chapter Eight

"Holly, there isn't a whole lot to that dress," John Scott looked at the beautiful elegant young woman who used to be his little girl. A wire of panic tightened around his heart as he looked at her.

"Oh, Daddy, there's enough to this dress. Why it comes up under my chin and reaches to the floor. Actually, it's rather conservative for this day and time." She turned around in the middle of the floor, the soft folds of her skirt swirling out to reveal the tiny straps of her shoes that arched across her feet.

"I meant the back, Holly," her father said, looking at the deep V that plunged toward her waist and revealed her straight smooth back. And he noticed that the high front clung to her rounded figure and emphasized her tiny waist.

"Oh, Daddy," she protested gently, giving him a quick kiss on the chin, "I've seen pictures of Mama in dresses that showed more than this."

She turned back to the old bureau wishing for the first time in her life that she had a full-length mirror. It had never seemed important before. She closed her eyes for a moment, trying to remember how the dress had looked on her in the triple mirror in the department store.

But even Holly's memory didn't do justice to the way the dress set off her beauty. The lustrous pale green color caught the green of her eyes and made her flawless complexion almost transparent. The design of the dress emphasized the smooth column of her neck and its gentle curve, while the long skirt molded her hips before it swirled to the floor. The sleeveless Empire bodice was cut high on the shoulders, which added to the graceful length of her arms.

"Holly," John Scott said slowly, "come on out on the porch and sit down. I want to talk to you a minute." He pushed the screen door open and went outside.

Holly smoothed her hair one last time and looked in the mirror to be certain it was still in place. She had looped the heavy tresses into a sleek intertwined knot at the base of her neck. Her only jewelry was a pair of very thin gold hoops that swung tantalizingly from her ear lobes. The ancient mirror was flecked and clouded with age and reflected back a dimmed image.

Sighing in resignation, she followed her father out onto the porch.

"Humph!" John Scott cleared his throat and took a long draw from his pipe.

"Oh, Daddy," she said anxiously, "you're not sorry that you said I could go, are you? Please don't be, because I couldn't have a good time knowing you didn't want me to go with Luke."

"No, Holly. It isn't that. I just don't want you to get your hopes up, child." The fragrance she knew and loved so well drifted from her father's pipe across the darkness to her.

"Don't worry. I'll have a wonderful time. I know I

will." Her eyes pleaded for him to be glad for her though it was too dark for him to know it.

"I meant don't get your hopes up about Luke Westford, Holly. He's not ordinary folks. He's used to that high-flying Washington crowd."

"The jet-set, Daddy. I know."

"And another thing. In a few days he'll be leaving here and Tannehill will be just another one of his long reports."

"I know that, too, Daddy." Her voice dropped to a whisper. She didn't need anyone to tell her Luke was from another world—a world of glamour and sophisticated women and all sorts of things she didn't know anything about.

"Then you go and have a good time, Holly, and let it stop there with Luke Westford."

"Yes, Daddy," she said obediently, wishing it could be that way and that she had some control over her heart.

John Scott looked at the big blue Catalina pulling into the space beside the cabin and spoke once more to Holly.

"You remember what I said."

"Yes, Daddy," she said as she turned and went back inside the cabin. She couldn't face Luke at that moment, not with her father's words ringing in her ears.

Her words to her father were almost like a lie, she thought, but she couldn't very well tell him that it was already too late. She couldn't tell him that the worst possible thing had already happened. She loved Luke Westford. She loved Luke, and all the admonitions and all the warnings in the whole world wouldn't make any difference.

As Holly went into the kitchen, she heard her father and Luke exchanging greetings on the front porch. She took a large pot from the refrigerator, carefully set it on the stove, and cut the flame on low. She turned another flame to medium under the coffee pot she had prepared earlier. Then she heard the front door open.

Out on the porch in the darkness, John Scott felt that wire about his heart tighten as he watched the scene in the living room unfold.

Luke stood just inside the door as Holly came back into the room. John Scott could see that they were in a special world of their own, a world in which he had no part. Although Luke was only telling Holly how lovely she looked, the quality of his voice revealed much more than that. Luke's eyes held a message that was unmistakable. And when John saw the beautiful light in his daughter's face, he felt as if he were observing a scene he had no right to see.

Luke's eyes never left Holly as she placed the roses he had brought into a vase and set them on a small table near the window.

They stopped on the porch to speak to John.

"The stew is on low, Daddy, and your coffee will be ready in a few minutes. Don't forget to feed the dogs."

"Buddy and Brandy will remind me," John Scott mustered up a laugh.

The way Luke held Holly's arm as they went down the steps and across the little bridge didn't make John Scott feel any better, either.

As the Catalina pulled slowly around the circle and out of sight, the older man sank into his rocker. He had not worked hard today, but he was exhausted. He sat in the darkness for a while thinking that he would do anything in the world to protect Holly from being hurt. But this was an affair of the heart and there was nothing he could do.

He slowly rose from the rocker and opened the

door for Brandy and Buddy to go into the house for supper. Then with almost painstaking care he slowly closed the front door.

Holly didn't look at Luke as they moved smoothly along the highway toward Birmingham. She didn't need to, for her mind was already filled with how elegant he looked. She remembered clearly how the length of his coat emphasized his height and shoulders, how the tiny tucks down his shirt front contrasted vividly with his rugged facial features, and how the midnight blue of his suit was a perfect complement to the lighter blue of his eyes.

Luke stopped for one of the endless traffic lights along the super highway.

"There's another way without so many lights," Holly said. "It's the back way across Shades Mountain. It takes longer, but it's a very scenic drive."

"We'll come back that way tonight. It'll give me a chance to see another part of the city."

Luke moved the car forward as the light changed. They lapsed again into a companionable silence as the neon glitter and a carnival of billboards paraded by, accompanied by the music from the Catalina tape deck.

Rectangular slabs of blue-pearl granite linked by white pylons, steel ribs overlaid with black marble, and anodized aluminum dominated the skyline of the city. To the left of the freeway the warm tones of the Civic Center's sweeping concrete planes extended for four blocks, while to the right, square bell towers, arched parapets and tall colonnades sprinkled the valley.

The Morris Avenue National Historic District was an interesting mixture of old dilapidated warehouses and turn-of-the-century buildings effectively renovated into nightclubs and restaurants. Gaslights and cobblestones gave Holly and Luke the impression they had stepped back into time when Victorian designers welded elaborate moldings, repetitive arches, and intricate relief panels.

The district was reminiscent of ladies in fashionable gowns, chivalrous gentlemen and horse-drawn carriages. Luke pulled Holly to his side under a train junction sign to allow a foursome to pass on the narrow sidewalk. Down the block, the lights of Diamond Jim's blazed in an 1890's motif.

They stood for a moment, savoring the atmosphere of a bygone era, then Luke escorted her up the steps of an old red boxcar.

Victoria Station, a popular restaurant noted for its unsurpassed cuisine, was located in one of the area's first former wholesale groceries. The entrance and foyer were a renovated railroad car, with plush red carpet and brightened by numerous brass railings and lamps. It was Holly's first excursion to a night spot and she was entranced by the new experience. Her eyes were wide and her cheeks flushed with the excitement that stirred inside.

Luke's hand under her elbow steered her across the room toward a handsome couple about Luke's age. As they drew nearer, Holly saw that the man, though expensively dressed, lacked Luke's vitality, and although the man's face was handsome, it lacked the image of strength in the face of the man at her side. The woman wore a floor-length mauve gown, split to the thigh, which Holly instinctively recognized as an original. The well-cut lines emphasized her voluptuous figure and the color set off her stylish dark hair. She was as glamorous as any fashion model Holly had ever seen in a magazine. Her carefully darkened lashes framed bored brown eyes, which impatiently surveyed her surroundings.

But when she saw Luke, her face became animated and her eyes expressive. With a brief glance, she coldly dismissed Holly; then she smiled again at Luke.

Holly's self-confidence faltered and she knew a brief moment of panic, remembering her own dress had been purchased at a discount department store. Then she thought of her father and how hard he had worked to buy her clothes and pay for her college expenses, and a steady smile came to her lips. Her chin lifted.

The introductions were casual, but Holly didn't miss the fact that Marta Shephens' acknowledgment was cool and distant. Nor did she fail to notice that Max Stephens was watching his wife intently.

Luke suggested that they ask for their reservations. As the four of them followed the hostess to a table, Marta clung to Luke's arm and left her husband to escort Holly.

Luke's skillful conversation countered Marta's barbed comments until the tension eased a little for Holly, but she was still painfully aware of the older woman's disdain.

When the waiter came for their order and Holly ordered fruit punch, Marta's carefully penciled brows rose a full half-inch.

"Why not milk?" she purred banefully.

"Now why didn't I think of that?" Luke laughed and looked across the table into Holly's eyes, sharing a moment with her that didn't include Marta or Max. "One of us has to drive home and I don't know the way."

Holly responded to Luke's jocose remark with a lovely smile that made Marta's deep red fingertips tense around her glass.

"Actually," Holly included Marta and Max in another

smile, "I had my limit before I left home. I don't drink."

Everyone laughed, but Marta's lips seemed thinner than Holly had first noticed.

The food was excellent and Holly ate almost as much as Luke or Max. The three of them devoured their huge servings of tender beef and enormous salads from the salad bar—down to the last mushroom. Marta hardly seemed to make a dent in her food.

Max, Marta, and Luke talked about old times and once or twice Luke cast an apologetic glance at Holly, but she seemed as interested in the conversation as the three of them and found the jokes just as amusing.

The station was filled to capacity, and a large boisterous group occupied a long table not far from theirs. At Marta's insistence they left and went to a quieter and more secluded club atop a south-side hotel. They all rode together in Max's car.

During the short ride, Marta dominated the conversation with references to times she had shared with Luke.

"Remember that weekend we spent in Daytona?" Marta asked, laughing as she turned from the front seat toward Luke.

"How could I forget it?" Luke answered. "Max and I swam far out to a sandbar on Saturday and on Sunday when we swam back out there, it was gone."

"And I almost didn't make it back," Max joined in the conversation as he pulled onto Twentieth Street.

"I think I prefer a cool relaxing swim in a wooded creek." Luke shared a secret smile with Holly.

As the car approached Five Points South circle, a white stone statue on a small platform in the center of the turnaround emerged in the glow of the street lights. A haunting kneeling figure, face turned to

Heaven, clutched a hat in his right hand, a Bible in his left. A fringed scarf was draped about his neck and trailed down his overcoat.

"Who's that?" Luke asked quietly, shifting his entire attention to Holly.

"Brother Bryan." Holly looked at the expressive face of the stone likeness. "There's a mission named for him in Birmingham. He literally used to take the coat off his back and give it away."

Marta clearly wanted to control the conversation. "What a lovely church." She pointed out a building to the right that resembled a Turkish mosque as she drew the attention back to her arena. The church was strikingly beautiful. The blue and purple stained glass windows, decorative facade, and embellished reliefs were perfect foils for an old gnarled tree on the front lawn.

"Yes," Holly agreed softly, unwilling to fight for Luke's attention.

Holly was glad when the car pulled under the awning. Luke's past was his business and she would rather not know of his relationship with the beautiful Marta Stephens.

The club was located in the penthouse of a hotel. An attractive foyer led from the elevator to double glass doors, which opened out onto a balcony or down a short hall to the main lounge.

They walked past the doors to the entrance of a large, dimly lit room. Small tables circled a dance floor. A three piece combo was playing a slow ballad. Bowls of candles flickered across the room and when Holly's eyes adjusted to the darkness, she could see there were very few empty tables.

Luke stepped back, catching Holly's hand in his, allowing Marta and Max to precede them into the room. He looked at Holly for a long moment, an unreadable, searching look that made her wonder if he were having second thoughts about inviting her and that perhaps he would have enjoyed the evening better if he were alone with his friends.

They were hardly seated at the tiny table when Marta reached over and put her hand on Luke's arm.

"It's been a long time since we danced together, darling," her voice was almost seductive.

"Yes, it has," Luke agreed, his face dark and expressionless in the shadows of the room. He rose from the table and guided Marta out onto the small dance floor.

Holly looked away from the two of them when she saw how closely they were dancing and glued her eyes on the glass of cola she held in her hand.

"Can't live with 'em, and can't live without 'em," Max muttered as he raised his drink, drained his glass, and signaled for the waiter to bring refills.

Holly looked up as a wry half-smile curved Max's lips. Her eyes reflected her concern.

"Don't pity me, Holly," he said, "I knew it when I married her. I just thought she would learn to love me."

"I don't pity you, Max." Holly's look was clear and steady. "A person can't hinge happiness on someone else. You have to find it within, or by giving of yourself to others. You don't find it by taking, or by expecting someone to measure up to your yardstick."

Max stared at Holly as he slowly lowered his glass to the table.

"Oh, I am sorry," she said. "I didn't mean to hurt you."

"So you don't pity me?" He turned the glass around in its own wet circular path.

"No. You're young and handsome and wealthy and—"

112

"But I'm not Luke Westford," Max said abruptly.

"You shouldn't try to be, either. Luke Westford isn't Marta's husband. You are. So be Max Stephens."

Max looked at Holly as if he were seeing clearly for the first time. "Until this moment I've never even considered the possibility of another woman in my life. I've been too occupied with the men in Marta's. I've looked, but never touched." He reached out and placed his hand over Holly's.

She slipped her fingers from his and took a sip from her glass.

"If this glass weren't empty, I'd drink a toast to old Luke out there. He's a darned lucky guy and I don't mean Marta." He disengaged her fingers from her glass. "I think I'd rather dance with you than toast Luke."

"I'd rather sit this one out," she said quietly.

Max half rose from his chair, exerting pressure on Holly's hand to follow his lead.

"No, Max," she repeated.

Max bumped his chair as he sat down, and, as he braced himself against the table, Holly wrestled her fingers from his grasp.

"Where's that waiter," Max mumbled, glaring at his empty glass.

Holly looked across the floor at the same time that Luke cast a disapproving glance in their direction. As the music ended, Luke and Marta walked toward them.

When Holly's eyes encountered Luke's across the table she noted a brooding darkness in the blue depths and the stern line of his mouth.

"We'll sit this one out, Max," Luke said in a voice unlike the tone Holly knew.

As if on cue, Max smiled, grabbed Marta's hand, and towed her toward the dance floor.

The waiter appeared with the drinks Max had ordered and precisely placed them in the proper order around the table. There was something in the way that Luke pulled the bills from his wallet that told Holly he was angry, that she had displeased him somehow.

"Is Max entertaining you with tall tales?" Luke inquired sardonically, as the waiter disappeared in the crowd.

"Luke..." Holly hedged, her eyes dropping to the tiny whipped stitches edging the double-tucks that ran up the front of his shirt.

He looked at Holly as he slipped his billfold back into his pocket.

"Was Max making a nuisance of himself?" Luke questioned bluntly.

"Nothing I couldn't handle," Holly said lightly, not wanting to mention the things that Max had said to her. Her fingers curved around the glass of Coke, her nails pale ovals against the darkness.

"Well, I couldn't handle the way he was looking at you," Luke spoke flatly. The anger she had seen a few minutes before was revealed in his voice.

"The way he was looking at me!" The words tumbled out as Holly remembered vividly the way Marta had looked at Luke since the beginning of the evening.

"Did your father give you a curfew?" Luke asked curtly.

"No!" Holly didn't add that her father probably never thought about it since she was going out with Luke. She would have bet her life that if she stayed out all night, John Scott wouldn't have a second thought about her honor. She knew the way her father felt about Luke. She saw it in his eyes every time he looked at Luke. She would have laughed, if she hadn't been so stung by Luke's abrupt words.

"He should have. We're leaving."

"If you thought I was such a child, why did you ask me to come?" Holly demanded fiercely. She saw Max and Marta emerging from the dancers on the floor.

"We'll talk about it later," Luke said, setting his untouched glass to the right.

"We never have to talk about it." Holly tilted her chin.

Luke told the Stephens they were leaving. "You can't be serious, Luke, darling. It's only ten!" Marta laughed as she raised her glass to her lips.

"I have an early day tomorrow. Sorry, Marta. Max, I'll be in touch. Enjoy the rest of your trip. We'll take a cab back to the car."

"We're leaving for Miami tomorrow," Max returned, and as Holly said good-night to them, Max rose and bowed slightly from the waist.

Luke guided Holly out into the lobby where two other couples were waiting for the elevator. He glanced down at the young woman at his side and saw the defiant angle of her chin, the gaiety gone from her face, the soft innocent mouth no longer curved in a smile. He steered her to the right, out double-glass doors, to a small open patio, and pulled her into the shadows.

"I think we'd better finish that talk now." He turned her to face him.

"I said we didn't need to talk about it." She looked up at him, her face composed and serenely sad, like a child who had known all along that she had expected too much of Christmas.

"We're going to talk anyway," he said firmly, his hands still holding her shoulders.

"Then let's get it over with!" She stepped back out of his grasp.

115

"We'll start with why I asked you to dinner tonight, Holly." He looked at her, slender and straight, silhouetted against the panorama of the city, the central figure in a great painting standing against the fiery glow of distant furnaces. "I didn't ask a child, Holly, I asked a lovely young woman to share what I hoped would be a beautiful evening."

"Then why are you so angry with me?" Her face lost a little of its composure, a tiny tremble flickering at the corner of her lips.

"I'm not angry with *you,* Holly. I'm angry with myself for subjecting you to Marta and Max. I guess I never really saw them clearly until I saw them beside you. And, I guess I thought time might change things for them."

"Oh, Luke, I haven't seen things too clearly tonight myself. You were very close to Max once, weren't you?"

"Yes." There was pain in his voice and Holly felt her heart go out to him for having been caught in that ancient geometric design, the eternal triangle.

Holly spoke with a serenity and wisdom beyond her years, "Luke, I think Max needs your friendship now more than he ever did. And as for Marta, remember that we can't always command the heart to perform and find that it will obey." The night breeze lifted a small curl from the coil at the base of her neck.

"Luke, I can still hear the music. The night isn't over."

The wind added violins to the melody that floated out over the balcony; the city added vibrant drumbeats; the night added soft flutes.

Luke and Holly walked across the tiled brick floor, fingers entwined, amid red shards of light that shattered and misted the floor. Whipping her dress about

116

their legs, the wind hurled moondust about the balcony until they were lost in a world of crimson and silver.

"Holly, could you still have that lovely evening—in spite of Marta and Max?"

"No, Luke, not in spite of them. Because of you."

It was all one great symphony of music, wind, and the rhythm of their hearts. Neither Holly nor Luke noticed when the sound of the little combo inside the club ceased, for they had heard a song that only those in love could hear.

She went into his arms and he held her close for a moment, his head bent, his forehead resting against her hair.

They stood motionless at the edge of the balcony on the embankment of a great city. Luke, a tall dark knight, and Holly, the maid who had gentled his heart.

On the horizon the red hot glow of furnaces soared into the black sky, filling the night with great spears of ruby, carmine, and wine.

His hands explored the soft contours of her face, then the length of those strong hands cupped her head with gentle strength. Her own hands found their way against his chest, above the tempo of his heart.

Luke slowly lowered his head until his mouth touched hers. Beneath an awning of flame-streaked sky, and against a skyline of burgundy, their hearts were forged, a blending together that would remain long after the molten steel in the distant furnaces had crumbled into dust.

Chapter Nine

It was only a kiss. Holly told herself that no less than a dozen times Sunday morning. Yet, she couldn't stop reliving those moments.

It was the first thing she thought about when she awoke. She dared not move at first, lest it was a dream that would take flight on the wings of morning.

Then it all came back vividly—she and Luke alone on a towering precipice above the city, surrounded by the night. The kiss had begun as gentle as a pale rosebud at the edge of her lips, then had unfolded into a brilliant flower with a thousand petals of fire. Luke's hands, which had cupped her unturned face, had traced a sublime path down her neck, around the base of her head, across her bare shoulders, and down her back. His arms had bound her to him with a strength that was almost frightening.

She got out of bed and went to the dim mirror above the bureau. Could she possibly look the same? The Holly of yesterday looked back at her. There was no evidence of his kiss, no marks where his caressing hands had touched her, no bruises where his arms had held her. Yet, she was not the same. She would never be the same again.

The scene was with her as she cooked breakfast and dressed for church. She wondered if she looked the same to her father or if he noticed her lack of appetite. But his very ordinary inquiries about her night out, and his, "Think I'll walk on up to church early," left her no doubt.

Even during the church service her mind drifted back to the minutes she and Luke had been alone in the car. On the way home, up the long Twentieth Street incline, they passed Vulcan with the city nestled in the valley below, and followed the scenic drive atop Shades Mountain. The furnaces were only a pink tinge in the distance. Then they went down into Roupe's Valley, through sleepy meadows dotted with small farm houses. The magic of the night wrapped them in the soft veil of enchantment.

And, she reflected, *that's why Luke kissed me. It was just his way of saying thanks for a beautiful evening.*

When they reached Tannehill, the park had been quiet, caught in a spell of silence and a moonbeam net that had been cast across the circle. Luke walked with her across the bridge to the steps of the cabin. He stood on the step below her, with only an inch or two to his advantage. Without warning, he leaned forward and brushed her cheek with a kiss—the kind he might have given her if her father and the whole world were watching.

As Holly came outside on the wooden steps of the church, she heard Buddy's familiar woof. He always waited a short distance from the church for the morning services to end and then ran ahead on the trail from the church to the cabin. He was anxious to

119

stretch his legs. "Yes, Buddy," she sighed aloud, "It was only a kiss."

It was only a kiss. Luke reminded himself of that fact again as he poured a cup of coffee from the nearly empty pot.

Luke Westford had been waging a battle with himself all morning. *She's too young,* he told himself. *It won't last,* he argued. *She doesn't know her own heart. Out of sight, out of mind. I can't take her with me and a week after I'm gone, it will all be over on her part. She's still in college. I'm nearly ten years older than she is.*

Nevertheless, after lunch he walked across the circle to the Scott cabin.

Perhaps, he admitted to himself, *it's time I talked a few things over with John Scott.*

Holly and John were on the porch. John sat in his favorite rocker, puffing leisurely on his pipe. The slow movement of the chair reflected the serenity of the afternoon. There were shadows beneath John's eyes and his skin seemed tinged with ashes. Luke wondered if John had looked that way yesterday, and he merely hadn't noticed. *Perhaps,* he thought as he glanced at Holly, *it's only because I see him against her beauty. A matter of youth and age—a division of innocence and experience.*

Holly was in the swing. She still wore the dress she had put on for church. She would have preferred jeans and shirt, but had made the usual concession to her father. It was a part of their Sunday ritual. For his part, John Scott put church first on Sundays and Holly second. He always managed a few minutes with her after lunch, even if it was his busiest day.

The navy pleats of Holly's dress spread across the

120

swing and ended in a fluted hem. The matching long-sleeved bodice was etched with a lace collar at the neck. Plain navy pumps completed the ensemble. Her head was bent, her eyes intent on the tiny stitches she was sewing in a small piece of linen, which was held securely between two oval hoops.

Holly's heart had begun an irrational quickening the moment she had seen Luke and Brandy start across the circle. To hide the color she felt sweeping into her face, she placed the hoops on the swing next to her and gave Brandy a friendly welcome.

Buddy rose from his spot at Holly's feet and stretched, his front paws extended, head down, his torso tapering sharply to powerful back legs. He reversed his stance and wagged a welcome.

"Hello, Luke," Holly said calmly, not raising her eyes from the lustered mahogany coat of his dog.

"Good afternoon, Holly. John."

"Join us, Luke," John Scott extended his usual enthusiastic welcome to Luke Westford.

Luke took the other rocker and Brandy settled down at Holly's feet with Buddy. The Irish setter crossed her front paws and looked up at Holly with silent wishful eyes.

Holly reached down and scratched Brandy briefly behind her amber-streaked ears.

"Would you like some coffee, Luke? I was about to bring Daddy some."

"Yes, thank you, Holly."

Their eyes met and Holly felt, unreasonably, that their lips had touched as well. She placed her needle-work on the swing and escaped to the kitchen.

As she poured the hot coffee, she tried to shut out the vision of Luke in her mind. *Can't I be without you for even a few minutes,* she grumbled. Luke Westford,

121

in his faded jeans and blue chambray shirt, was the most disquieting man in the world. She girded herself for the task of acting normal, for the simple act of sitting on her own front porch.

However, when she returned, Luke and her father were engaged in a game of checkers. Neither man saw the delicate brows lift in surprise.

It turned out to be a rather pleasant interlude. From her vantage point in the swing, Holly could observe the game between stitches. She found herself trying to analyze what it was that made Luke Westford so disturbingly attractive. Handsome became a pallid word when used to describe the carved planes of his face, the straight nose, the well-formed mouth. It was much more than the way he looked. It had something to do with his air of confidence and with his ability to put everyone at ease with such little effort. She couldn't imagine any woman not being affected by him.

That bit of reverie turned the tables of her thoughts. Of course, there must be women in his life. True, he hadn't talked about any particular one, but that didn't mean there wasn't one. Unable to dispel that thought, she tried to focus her attention on the green satin stitches which were forming the branches of a Tannehill pine. She slowly made a small stitch in the linen and secured the knot.

As Luke spread the checkers for another game, John Scott pulled his watch from his pocket and looked at his daughter.

"Holly, you haven't forgotten about the wedding, have you?"

"No, Daddy. I'll go up to the church now and make sure everything is in order."

She folded the linen around the hoops and went into the house. As she changed her dress for jeans and shirt, she mustered up her courage to invite Luke to go with her. But her newfound bravery deserted her at the front door, so she spoke through the screen.

"Would you like to walk up to the church, Luke?"

His eyes asked a silent question as he looked at her attire.

"Oh, I'm not going for the wedding. I have to see that the church is swept and dusted."

Luke looked at her thoughtfully before he declined. "I think I'll try one more game of checkers, Holly."

"There's more coffee on the stove," she said quickly, to hide her disappointment. "How about you, Brandy? Would you like a walk with me and Buddy?"

After a nod from Luke, the Irish setter jumped to her feet and followed Buddy through the cabin and out the back door. When the three of them were out of hearing range of the cabin, Holly spoke to the dogs, her voice wistful with regret.

"You see, it was only a kiss."

As Holly, Buddy, and Brandy disappeared from view, Luke pondered the move John Scott had made on the board. John leaned back in his rocker and puffed on his pipe.

"What's on your mind, Luke?" John looked through a haze of smoke at the younger man.

"Holly."

"I figured as much."

The two men looked at each other across the board, the silence heavy between them.

"John, I know that Holly—" Luke was interrupted by the slam of a truck door at the road. Two men in park uniforms had gotten out of the truck and were walking toward the cabin.

"Sorry, Luke," John Scott rose to meet his workers, "We'll talk later."

As Holly cleaned the simple wooden place of worship, the turmoil in her mind subsided. The old Tannehill Church was a favorite sanctuary, its solitude a comfort to her as it had been to many others in the past.

When she was troubled about a problem, Holly would often spend time on the steps of the "Church in the Wildwood," as it was affectionately called. From the porch overlooking the park, faraway foothills seemed to melt into the horizon. And, just as surely, her problems always seemed to melt away after she had placed them in the proper perspective before the Lord.

She swept the wooden floors and straightened the hymnbooks, then polished the carved wooden altar rail and the stand where the large pulpit Bible was kept. She dusted every pew, leaving her favorite job of polishing the pianos until last. The church boasted two pianos, one on each side of the platform, and they sounded almost like grands when played properly. The old uprights were very tall and embellished with scrolls and curlicues that took a very long time to dust. And Holly dusted every little crevice until not a speck of dust remained.

When her work was finished, Holly slipped into a back pew. She sat quietly for a few minutes, listening to Buddy and Brandy barking at a bird taunting them from a low branch. She closed her eyes as another vision of Luke assailed her mind.

As if summoned by her thoughts, the door opened and Luke slid into the pew beside her.

She raised her defenses. After all, she had let them

down and now she suffered the emotional turmoil that had resulted.

"I suppose you're wondering why anyone would want to have a wedding in an old place like this?"

"That thought hadn't occurred to me," he said quietly, surveying the rustic interior of the sanctuary.

"Then I guess you're thinking that the music won't be appropriate since there's only two very old pianos."

"I don't object to piano music for weddings," he answered with mock sobriety.

"But the church is too small?"

His mouth lifted in a faint smile. "Are you angry because I didn't accept your invitation?"

"You think I'm very transparent, don't you?"

"Back to your old tricks, spitfire?" the smile faded as he reached for her hand, which had been lying deceptively still in her lap.

She tried to elude him, but his fingers captured hers.

"I think the church is perfect for Tannehill. An old white church with pointed windows, a traditional roof, and a white bell tower is a fine place for any wedding. And, yes, you are transparent."

His hand closed tighter over hers as she tried to free herself.

Holly's voice was deliberately steady and cool as she answered. "This church was built in 1905. It was abandoned for fifteen years before it was relocated here."

"I don't think you have your mind entirely on the church, Holly. Can we at least agree on that?" He drew her toward him, turning her palm against his heart.

Oh, she thought, *there won't be any place I can go after he's gone that won't be sharp with the memory of him. Not even the church.* Aloud, with a voice still amazingly cool, she said, "We added the bell and windows."

125

As his other arm drew her against him she stopped resisting. His mouth was only a kiss away.

At that moment, a truck rumbled up the steep hill and stopped at the church door.

"The flowers are here." Her breath touched his mouth. "Right on time."

"Perhaps just in time," Luke said lightly, releasing her from his arms. He pulled her to her feet and they walked from the cool interior of the church out into the brilliant Tannehill sunshine.

A young man just a little older than Holly was unlocking the back doors of a truck. He turned as they walked down the steps. He looked first at Holly, an unmistakable light springing into his eyes, then at Luke with a questioning gaze.

Holly briefly introduced Luke to Larry Jacobs, and she and Luke helped carry the flowers into the church. White wicker baskets overflowing with white ruffled gladioli and painted daisies filled the small aisle. Tall polished wooden candleholders stood like honor guards at the back door, waiting to be summoned to their places on the altar.

"Could you stay and help me with the candles, Holly?"

Larry Jacobs sported a mop of curly brown hair, an athletic physique, and a ready smile. If Holly missed the hopeful expectation in his voice, Luke didn't.

"Everything always looks beautiful when you arrange it, Larry. You don't need me. I guess I'll just walk on back with Luke." The way she said it almost took the sting out of her rejection—but not entirely, Luke noted, as he silently gave Holly a plus for tact.

"See you next time, Holly," Larry called as they started down the path.

Brandy and Buddy disbanded their game of chasing

birds to accompany Holly and Luke down the hill. The dogs bounded with gusto into piles of accumulated pine straw and mounds of fallen leaves.

"What made you decide to come up to the church, Luke?" Holly asked, unable to quash her curiosity any longer.

"Your father had work to do. Two workers rescued him from my checker playing."

"Oh, so I turn out to be the lesser of three evils?"

"You turn out to be the most argumentative woman I've ever met."

"What do you expect from someone who plays second fiddle to a checker game?" She couldn't suppress a little laugh.

"I had something to talk to your father about. It wasn't all checkers. Will that help your wounded pride?"

"Yes. So much, in fact, that I'll offer you another cup of coffee when we get home."

"Truce offering?"

"Truce."

The hill became steeper and Holly began to run. "Beat you home," she said, dashing ahead on the narrow path.

But when the path widened, Luke caught her hand and they ran together down the slope, across the road and down the path into the back door of the cabin. They stopped to catch their breaths before going inside.

"I could have won if you hadn't held me back," she said flippantly.

The look Luke gave her made her want to retract her statement, but she quickly thought of a way out of it. "Truce, I remember."

She opened the door and went inside, followed by Luke and the dogs.

"While we're in a state of truce, I'll press my advantage," Luke said blandly. When Holly stopped and turned to look at him, he continued. "Would you and John watch Brandy tomorrow and tomorrow night? I've got to go down to Montgomery."

"Yes, of course," she said lightly, but she turned away so that he couldn't see the disappointment in her eyes.

Luke followed her into the living room.

"We're back, Daddy," she called as she walked to the front door. There was no response, so she opened the door and looked out. Her father was nowhere to be seen. She closed the screen and turned around right into Luke's arms.

He pulled her against him, molding their lengths together in a movement that was a bewildering combination of roughness and tenderness.

"Did I forget to tell you? Your father went down to the furnace." Luke's eyes belied the lightness of his words.

His mouth had barely touched hers when the sound of three car doors jarred through the cabin. He held her tightly for a brief moment and transferred his kiss to just below her ear.

"This is obviously no place to get away from it all. It's more like Grand Central Station," he muttered reluctantly. He released her and walked out on the porch, with Brandy at his heels. He snapped on Brandy's leash, walked out to the three men, and paused briefly to speak to them.

Holly leaned against the wall just inside the cabin door, arms crossed over her hammering heart. She heard Luke tell her father he would be in Montgomery for a day and night. Then she heard Brandy's name before the rest of the conversation was lost to her. When she looked out the door, Luke and Brandy were far out into the circle. Her father, Clarence Warner, and Alton Turner were slowly making their way across the bridge.

"Holly," John Scott called, "look who I ran into down at the furnace."

"Hello," Holly greeted her father's lifetime friends, "You haven't been to see us for so long we thought you'd forgotten about us. Come on in and I'll put on some fresh coffee."

"Hullo, Holly," Clarence hitched up his pants as he came up the steps.

"Pretty as ever," Alton grinned, spinning his hat into the swing.

"Holly, put on that coffee while I finish up down at the furnace. Then I can spare a few minutes for a visit before I go over to the mill." John Scott turned toward the steps.

Clarence spoke as he set the checkers up for a game. "Thought we'd come out and visit a spell and get away from it all."

Holly smiled to herself as she turned and went into the cabin.

Chapter Ten

"I'll pick you up at seven," Charles reminded Holly as he stopped the car in front of the cabin.

"Pick me up at seven?" she repeated absently, gathering her books from the back seat.

"The film series, Holly. Remember?"

"Oh, yes." Holly remembered with a jolt. Charles had asked her to the series weeks ago when the fall activities schedule had been posted. At the time, it had seemed like a wonderful idea. Now it was impossible.

"I can't go with you, Charlie," Holly said, shifting her books to one slim jean-encased hip as she reached for the car door with her other hand.

"Wait, Holly," Charles's voice raised a full octave as he slid across the seat and caught the door before it slammed.

Holly stood there, impatiently juggling the books from arm to arm.

"Did Luke Westford ask you not to go out with anyone else, Holly?"

"No, of course not, Charlie."

"Well, I know you don't have a date with him tonight because I saw his setter over here this morning. That means he's gone and won't be back until tomorrow. Right?" He reached back, turned off the motor, pulled the keys from the ignition, and slipped the ring over a finger.

"Charlie," an apology was threaded through the syllables of his name.

"Have you got a date with someone else?"

"No, Charlie, it isn't that either."

"I'm not letting you off, Holly. A date's a date. If you had forgotten about the festival and had a date with Luke that would be one thing, but this is something else. You've got no excuse. So,...I'll pick you up at seven."

They stared at each other. It was the closest they had come to a serious argument in all their years of friendship. It wasn't a pleasant feeling.

Holly stood there, undecided. She had never known anything to make so much difference to Charles.

"I'll be ready, Charlie," she heard herself saying. And to herself, she added, *and you're right about one thing. There are no promises between me and Luke. We have no holds on each other.*

Still, as she slipped the oriental rose silk dress over her head, she was not able to shake the nagging thought that even though there were no promises between her and Luke, there was something awry about her date with Charles. And, as she looped the fabric tie about the elasticized waist, she kept remembering that she had promised Luke to help watch Brandy. Then, after fastening the white enameled costume bracelet on her arm, she walked through the house to the telephone. She stood trying to think how she could call Charles and ask for a rain check. She wanted to make him understand why she couldn't go, but before she dialed the number, she heard his car. Charles was thirty minutes early.

131

Holly had always enjoyed the film festivals in other years, sometimes with Charles, sometimes with another date. But this festival was different. She couldn't think of anyone except Luke.

And none of the frantic chases, custard pies, and spontaneous confusion of the Keystone Kops, or the humorous chicanery of W. C. Fields made any difference to Holly's heart. Halfway through the first film she almost said aloud what was persistently whirling about the merry-go-round of her mind. *What am I doing here? This doesn't feel right. Only being with Luke is right.*

But at intermission, it was Charles who made the move. He had conceded defeat. "Would you like to go home, Holly?" he asked gently, as they walked up the aisle to the concession stand.

"Yes, Charlie, I would." She gave him a grateful smile.

Back on the porch of the cabin, Holly breathed a sigh of relief, then suffered a moment of regret.

"Charlie, I'm sorry about missing the last film. I know how much you were looking forward to Bogey."

"Don't be too sorry, Holly," he smiled and said offhandedly. "I've seen it twice before."

Just then Buddy came to the front door. Holly pulled the screen door open and let him out on the porch, but Brandy was nowhere to be seen. Suddenly Holly realized Luke must have come, taken Brandy, and left, and she wasn't able to hide the disappointment that surged through her.

There was a moment of silence as Charlie turned the car keys around his finger twice. His smile was replaced by a serious expression.

"You're in love with him, aren't you, Holly?"

Holly expelled her breath on another long sigh.

132

How could she admit to Charles what she had tried so desperately to hide?

"You don't have to say anything, Holly," Charles said, the smile back, this time a wistful curve to his mouth.

"Good night, Charlie."

"Good night," Charles repeated. Then in a twangy nasal drawl, he added, "my little chickadee."

Holly's smile was his reward as he turned and tipped his imaginary hat and crossed the little bridge to his car.

Late Wednesday afternoon, after an early supper, Holly sat on the porch with her father and absent-mindedly made stitches on the linen square. A blue L, exactly the shade of Luke's eyes, slowly curved about the trunk of a graceful pine, then a W joined it, against the faint outline of a distant mountain. Holly admitted the design was a bit fancy for a man, but she liked it and she hoped it would please Luke. It was just a matter of days before he left Tannehill and the handkerchief was to be a good-bye gift.

The sun dropped behind the trees and shades of dusk dimmed the tiny stitches. Holly looked across the circle as she wove the needle into the material and folded the square about the hoops. She had hoped Luke and Brandy would come across the circle for an evening visit, but she had not seen Luke since Sunday.

Night brought with it sweet memories, and Holly was engulfed by longing to be with Luke. She went into the cabin and walked through the kitchen, then back to the front door. Then she went back into the kitchen, took the broom from its niche beside the refrigerator and began to sweep. In no time at all she had worked her way into the living room.

"Holly, what are you doing?" Her father's rocker stopped its rhythm.

"Cleaning the house," she said, sweeping behind the door for the third time.

"Tomorrow's a school day," he reminded her, looking out across the dark circle to Luke's camper. His face was a study of thoughtfulness.

"I know, Daddy, but you know how I like to have things straightened up before I leave the house." At least that part was true, she conceded.

"Humph!" Her father puffed an extra time as the chair resumed its meter.

An hour later, whiffs of sweet-smelling pound cake drifted through the cabin and twirled tantalizingly about the porch.

"Humph!" John Scott listened to the sounds of Holly washing the cake pan and mixing bowl. He rubbed his chin in a pondering gesture.

"Daddy, would you like some cake? You know its best when it's hot." Holly called from the front room.

"Smells mighty good, Holly." John Scott rose from his rocker and held the door open for Buddy. The three of them went into the little kitchen.

"You expecting Luke?" John Scott took a bite out of his second piece of cake.

"No." Holly hoped her father didn't notice that most of her cake disappeared under the table where an expectant Buddy waited in his habitual supper pose.

"'Pears to me that the smell of this cake would have Luke and most everybody else in the park knocking down our door." John Scott picked up a large crumb on the table and dropped it to Buddy.

"Oh, Daddy," Holly laughed in spite of her doldrums. "It isn't that good. It's just your favorite."

"It is good." Her father looked as if he were contemplating a third piece. "Since it looks like Luke isn't coming over, maybe you and Buddy ought to take him a piece."

Holly glued her eyes to the table, wondering if she had heard her father right. Had he really suggested she ought to go over to Luke's camper? That was the one place she had set as off-limits, even if only in her own mind. It was a defense mechanism she had invented for herself, a last barrier she was not prepared to cross. Yet, it was a barrier that she longed to break tonight. She worded her answer carefully.

"Well, I suppose I could," she ventured, "but Luke must be awfully busy not even to drop by for an evening visit." She had left herself a way out. It was a decision she couldn't face at the moment.

Her father pushed back his chair and picked up his coffee mug.

"Think I'll sit on the porch a spell before bedtime, Holly. Don't reckon there will be many more nights as warm as this one, and then there won't be any more sitting on the porch till spring."

"You're right about that, Daddy," Holly said as she gathered up the two small plates, the forks, and her mug.

Then she was alone in the little kitchen again—alone with her thoughts of Luke. She ran too much hot water in the sink, stirred the suds too vigorously, and washed and rinsed the too-few dishes too long. It was over in a moment.

You've won, Luke, she said to herself. Then she walked to the front door.

"Daddy, I guess I will take Luke's cake over before it gets completely cold." *If Daddy offers the slightest objection, I won't go,* she thought. *Perhaps he'll say it's too late to go now, or he's thought better of it and Luke can have his cake tomorrow. He might even say he'll walk over with me.*

But John Scott didn't say any of those things. He didn't even stop rocking. He just said the same words to Holly he had said so many times before.

"Remember, tomorrow's a school day, Holly."

As she turned to go back to the kitchen, her father added, "Take yourself a piece of cake. Maybe you'll find your appetite over that way."

The lights from Luke's camper were obscured by drawn shades. The night seemed even darker as the wind blew a cumulous cloud across the half moon. Holly admired the well-defined white, fluffy mountains of vapor in the sky illuminated by the hidden light. She did not see Luke sitting in the screened-in-patio until she opened the flap and stepped inside. She was disconcerted when she realized he had been there all the time watching her cross the circle. Her carefully rehearsed greeting lodged in her throat. She waited there silently while Buddy went to Luke and greeted Brandy.

"Good evening, Holly." Luke's voice had a sensual quality in the darkness, an unintentional inflection that Holly knew came natural to him. He stood, almost touching the canopy.

"Hello, Luke," she rejoined. She stooped to stroke Brandy, who had come begging for her share of attention. Holly didn't look up as she explained her visit.

"I brought you some cake." The excuse sounded so flimsy when she spoke the words aloud. She wished she hadn't come. She sensed a skeptical uplifting of his brows. "It's better when it's warm," she continued, "if you have an appetite for it." Did his brows rise another notch, she wondered? After all, she was practically inviting herself into his camper.

136

"Why don't you join me?" he replied.

What did I expect—, she chided herself, *Luke to turn me down?* Well, it was too late now to back out. Luke fastened the door of the patio to keep the dogs inside and with a sweep of his hand motioned for Holly to precede him into the camper. He reached around her to open the door.

The camper was well-arranged and extraordinarily neat. To Holly's right was a curved, rust-colored couch that made an attractive living area in the front end. A little to the left was a small table with two captain's chairs covered in rust and black figured fabric. Directly across was a modern kitchen with a small double sink. In the back she could see a bed partially hidden by the bath on one side and a small closet on the other. Plain, but attractive, rust curtains were drawn back to reveal shades bordered in black. There were no clothes thrown about and no dirty dishes in the sink.

"Very nice," she commented, glancing at Luke. His face was an impervious mask.

There was a long, terrible silence between them. Then Luke abruptly turned and squarely faced her.

"Why are you here, Holly?" he asked harshly.

"Because..." she spoke haltingly. How could she answer that question. In the pause that followed, she sensed rather than saw the anger in him. "I think—I think I'd better go, Luke."

He blocked her way, his eyes dropping to the slim jeans and pink, crew-necked pullover, then back to her face.

"I'll rephrase that question, Holly. Why aren't you out with Charlie."

"Is that why you're angry with me, Luke? Because of Monday night?" Her eyes finally met his. "Is that

137

why I haven't seen you for three days."

"I have no right to be angry with you, Holly. You're free to go out with Charlie or anyone else."

"But you are upset about it, aren't you? Why didn't you give me a chance to explain instead of avoiding me?"

"There's nothing to explain."

"There's everything to explain if it matters to you, Luke."

He looked at her, a pulse visibly throbbing at the edge of his jaw.

"Does it, Luke?" Holly stood her ground.

"Yes," he admitted slowly. "It does."

"Luke,…" she began, her voice heavy with relief. "I had forgotten all about that date with Charlie. He asked me to a film festival back in early September. Back…" she paused, "back before I met you." She looked at him for a long moment, then continued. "He reminded me of it Monday afternoon. There was no way to let you know or no way to tell you."

That grim mask he wore began to fade; that tiny beating pulse in his jaw receded.

"When I saw that you had already come for Brandy…" For another long moment, the scales swayed. Holly felt as if her very existence was in the balance. "Luke…Luke, I had a miserable time."

The last trace of anger left him, replaced by a rueful smile. "So did I," he said.

Luke reached out and almost touched her face, then as if on second thought, turned and took the old coffee pot from the stove.

"I think we'd better have that cake now, Holly," he said, rinsing out the grounds and refilling the pot.

She stood there watching the efficiency with which

he worked, then sat in one of the captain's chairs at the table.

Luke turned the flame on high and sat down opposite her. For Holly, it was a strange moment. Everything seemed changed since she had last seen him. It was as if she were on a highway with no speed limit, still worse, with no brakes on her car.

"Do you keep your house as neat as this camper, Luke?" she asked, smiling to break the feeling of constriction about her heart.

"No, but then there's no need. It's a big rambling place and you don't notice a few things out of pocket. This is cramped quarters and any mess would only add to the lack of space."

"Tell me about your house," she prodded, knowing it would be a little glimpse of him she hadn't had before—a way to think of him when he was gone.

"There's not much to tell." He leaned over and turned the flame under the coffee down to low. "It's a two-story farm house. There's a big stone chimney, a sun porch which faces south, and an old-fashioned parlor with a high ceiling. A wide staircase almost fills the front hall."

As Luke looked at Holly, a fleeting vision of her in the parlor flashed into his mind. He saw her fragile beauty against the dark walnut panels, her radiant smile in the sunlight, which poured through the glass windows of the sun porch, her pale hair against the burnished wood of the old four poster. Something of his thoughts was transmitted to Holly when he spoke. She looked away from the expression in his eyes.

"It sounds lovely, Luke."

"There was enough room in the house for grandfather's twelve children."

"Twelve children!" Holly pondered that for a moment, her eyes on the design in the table top. Then she asked, "With so many heirs, how did you end up with the house?"

"Believe it or not, there were eleven girls and my father. Each of them received a dowry, and he got the old homestead," Luke's brief laughter eased the tension that seemed to be building between them.

"And, what's it like outside?" Holly prompted.

"The house is white. A porch curves around from front to back. The soil is rich and dark. Corn, soybeans, oats, and hay grow without too much cultivating. There's one thing you'd especially like, Holly. Many of the farm houses in Iowa only have a row of trees that serve as a windbreak, but the homestead is in a wooded area. Oak, elms, hickory, maples, willows, and cottonwoods grow along the stream that winds behind the house—a rare thing these days. Sometimes you can glimpse a white-tailed deer from the porch. My grandfather set aside that portion of the land for a reserve."

Why, he speaks of his home like Daddy talks about Tannehill, she thought. Some men seem to put down roots just like trees, and become a part of the earth. She looked directly into his eyes.

"It sounds as beautiful as Tannehill."

"It is—different, but somehow the same."

There was a moment of silence, then Luke rose from the chair and took two cups and saucers from the little cabinet. Holly watched him pour the coffee and set it on the table. As she unwrapped the cake, a whippoorwill warbled a night song outside the window above the sink.

"At home, it's the goldfinch and cardinal, Holly, or the cry of a meadowlark."

Her father had been right. Her appetite returned.

The cake was delicious, and as Luke told her about Iowa, she relaxed in the spell of his voice.

She could almost see the prairie grass, wild flowers, and lilies, almost feel the touch of wild roses, asters, and indigo, almost taste the cold water from the spring. His words sent her sledding down a snow-banked hill, showed her wintry, steel-gray skies, and swept her around the bend of the frozen creek on ice skates.

Holly was reluctant to return to reality, even Tanne-hill, admitting to herself that whenever she was with Luke there seemed to be a magic about it. More and more her life was made up of wanting to be with Luke. Yet, when she was with him, she dreaded the time when they would have to be parted.

But time would not stand still, so she refused Luke's offer of a third cup of coffee and stacked her dishes with his.

"I'll take care of those later, Holly," he said, reaching for the dishes and encountering her fingers.

Holly almost dropped the dishes at his touch. "No, I'll do it," she insisted and quickly slipped from her chair and placed the dishes in the sink.

When the few pieces were dried and stacked in the cabinet, Holly made a final unnecessary sweep with the dishcloth about the counter, wiping nonexistent crumbs and spots from the tile. When there was no more room even for pretense, she turned around. It was time to go—she couldn't put it off any longer.

Luke still sat at the table. As her eyes met his, she was startled by the fire in the blue depths.

"You shouldn't have come here, Holly." His voice was suddenly harsh and cold, a paradox to the blue flame of his eyes.

"I know, Luke. But Daddy suggested that I bring you

141

some cake." Her words sounded uncertain and afraid. "It didn't take a lot of persuasion."

She looked at his finely shaped mouth, a mouth that belonged to a man of passion, who underneath all that polish and diplomacy had a heart waiting to release its love.

"Why would your father do that, Holly? He ought to know better."

"I guess Daddy figures he knows you pretty well, Luke." Her voice dropped to a whisper. "He did it because he knew how desperately I wanted to see you."

Holly was acutely aware of herself in this moment. She was aware of her blood surging through her body—of the terrible attraction of this man—and of the longing which flooded her mind and body like the song of the forest filling the valley.

"Holly." Luke spoke her name as she had never heard it spoken before.

She walked to him, slowly, as if drawn by invisible threads. She stood before him for a long moment, then her hands touched his shoulders.

The whole evening had been a prelude to this moment, an overture before the symphony.

Almost unwittingly, he reached for her, his hands sliding about her waist and up across her back. As he rose from his chair, her arms entwined about his neck and the curtain of her hair fell forward to touch him. Her lips brushed the hard planes of his face as he lifted her from the floor. He held her against him, molding them into one figure. Then he released the constriction of his arms until her toes touched the floor.

He bent his head to her, kissing her eyes, the edge of her mouth, the hollow of her neck, until her lips turned to his. His mouth finally met hers.

It was a long shattering moment of intimacy and intensity. The ascendant song of Tannehill sang in Holly's heart as she returned his kisses with the knowledge love had given her. Her lips, young and soft, moved under his; her body, young and pliant, pressed to him; her heart, young and unknowing, answered him.

Holly, yielding to her love for Luke, tasted the dark red wine of desire and perceived the mystery of love.

Luke swung her into his arms and looked down at the pale beauty of her face. She was a fragile flower of the forest, a vulnerable woman of the woodland. He caught her closer to his heart and kissed the closed eyes, the fluttering pulse at the base of her throat, the trembling lips.

Abruptly, he turned and carried her back through the little kitchen, and, holding her with one arm, opened the door of the camper, then stepped with her into the Alabama night.

"I'll walk you home," Luke said, gentleness in his voice as he lowered her to her feet.

He didn't hold her hand as they crossed the great circle, nor did he kiss her good night. It was almost as if Holly had dreamed the past few minutes. But she knew that it was true, for Luke had bound more than her slender body with his arms. He had bound her heart, and her mind. She knew she would never be the same; the invisible marks of his love would always be there.

They stopped in the shadows at the bridge. John Scott was in his rocker on the porch.

"Luke, I think Daddy knows you better than I do," Holly said.

He spoke from the shadows as he turned to go.

"Perhaps better than I know myself."

Chapter Eleven

Luke crossed the circle to the Scott cabin, with Brandy bounding to and fro and dashing to investigate a falling leaf or sniff the path of a long-departed field rat. He took the steps of the cabin two at a time and knocked on the front door. He was greeted by the aroma of fresh coffee and the voice of John Scott.

"Door's open!" the older man called.

Luke walked through the front room to the kitchen, glancing into Holly's room as he passed. The small single bed was smoothly spread with a beautiful patchwork quilt, "A Trip Around the World." He smiled to himself thinking that was ironic since Holly had never been any farther from home than Mobile, Alabama.

"Good morning, John."

"Morning, Luke. Pull yourself up a chair. Coffee's on the stove."

They talked about the park, the proposed enlargement of the area, and finally the weather, all the while both of them knowing Luke hadn't mentioned the real reason he had come.

"It's Holly you've come to talk about, Luke, so let's get on with it."

"All right, John," Luke answered.

John Scott reached for his pipe and stuffed the tobacco in it with slow deliberation. After searching his pockets for a match and holding a light to the tobacco, he puffed rapidly.

"I thought that talking things over with the father was out of style, Luke. Specially in that high-flying crowd you're used to running with."

"Yes, to both of those, John," Luke met the older man's gaze with steady eyes.

"You don't have to ask me, Luke." John Scott reflected a moment, his eyes shifting to look out at the last of the fall roses, then up to the hills above the trees as if he had suddenly remembered something from the past. "Or Holly either, for that matter. Reckon all you've got to do is crook your little finger and she'll follow you right to the end of the earth."

"I know that, John," Luke admitted quietly.

"You ask *her* yet?"

"No."

"How about some more coffee, Luke?" John rose and went to the stove and returned with the pot. He poured Luke's cup first, confident that silence meant consent, then refilled his own. Slowly, almost haltingly, he returned the pot to the flame.

"Heady stuff. Strong. Guess that's what makes a man or woman able to leave mother and father and make a life anew. I saw it the first night you got here right in this house. Almost like you two had discovered you were the only two people left in the whole world."

"You didn't try to head it off, John. Maybe you should have."

"You mean try to keep you two apart?"

"You did suggest that Holly show me the park. Remember?"

"I had my reasons. Besides I knew from the first there wasn't going to be any keeping you apart." The sweet odor of the pipe wafted through the house. "You know how youngsters are—forbid them something and it just makes it all the sweeter. Like snitching mama's cookies off the kitchen windowsill."

"I never meant for this to happen, John."

"Reckon I know that, too. I never intended for it to be a big forest fire myself. Guess I figured those sparks might just die out after a while—at least on your side anyway, Luke."

"I'm not talking about marriage now, John. I know how young Holly is—too young. I'm not even talking about any promises on her part, not with her last year in college still to go. She could change her mind two days after I'm gone."

John Scott laughed, the first humor of the afternoon. "Don't you count on Holly changing her mind, Luke. So, if you're not certain of yourself, you'd best hold your peace."

"I'm sure, John," Luke said, his gaze meeting that of John Scott. "And if Holly still feels the same next summer, after she graduates—"

The sudden clatter of John Scott's cup against the wooden floor ended Luke's words in mid-sentence. John's hand that only a moment ago had held the cup so firmly, now clutched spasmodically at his chest, then moved to his neck and down his left arm. His face contorted as if a great weight was compressing his chest.

"John!" Luke rose from his chair to assist the older man.

"Pocket...." John muttered, bowing his head against the stabbing pain that was piercing his chest like a knife.

In a continuous movement Luke secured the small tablets and placed one under John Scott's tongue. He held his older friend in the chair while the pain subsided, the coronary vessels dilating and allowing the life-saving blood to flow again. Two, then three, minutes elapsed, and some of the pain left John's face. His fingers relaxed.

"Worst...."

"Don't talk, John," Luke cautioned. "Just rest."

"Worst one yet, Luke. Sorry, I didn't mean for you to be around when this happened."

They sat silently in the kitchen until Luke was certain the attack had passed. Then he returned the small container of nitroglycerine tablets to John.

"You ought to be taking it easy, John. You have no business tramping the hills, or pushing against the wind, or being under any kind of strain. Don't you know that?"

"I've been slowing down, Luke. That's why I asked Holly to show you around."

"Not slow enough, John." He looked at a face which seemed painfully tired and worn after the ordeal of the past few minutes. "Angina?"

"Yes."

"And your heart?"

"Reckon it'll last a while longer."

"I want it straight, John."

"Advanced arteriosclerosis," John Scott said slowly, the mask he had worn so well for the past weeks falling away, a beaten, tired man revealed. He looked at Luke. "Don't tell Holly. Promise me you won't."

"John—"

"That's all I've got, Luke. It's all that's holding me together. Don't take that away from me." Desperation filled the eyes of a tormented man.

"All right, John."

"I got your word, Luke?"

"You've got my word."

John Scott held out his hand, but it wasn't just a handshake; it was a clasp of a thousand words. It told Luke how much John Scott needed that promise and how much he needed Luke's added strength to draw upon.

"Think I'll go lie down a while, son," John Scott rose slowly from the chair and with Luke's assistance walked haltingly to the bedroom.

"I'd better call your doctor," Luke said as he lifted John's leaden legs up on his bed.

"No, there's nothing he can do. The pain is gone now. I'll have a park ranger drive me into town tomorrow." John Scott closed his eyes. "Luke, you and Holly...have my blessings."

Luke waited until he heard steady breathing before he let himself quietly out of the cabin.

That afternoon was anguish for Luke Westford. He weighed every alternative, thought of every angle, considered every possibility, and each time he ended up precisely where he had started.

How could he speak of his love to Holly without committing himself to her? How could he make plans that might come to pass in John Scott's last days? How could he take Holly away from her father when his remaining time was so uncertain? And if Holly did go with him, and her father's time was short, could Holly ever forgive herself for leaving her father when he needed her so?

Later in the day as Luke started across the circle to check on John Scott, he saw John slowly walking toward the camp store. Luke expelled his breath on a long sigh. At least John seemed to have recovered for the present.

Instead of going back to the camper, Luke turned toward Mud Creek, Brandy at his heels. Luke walked the banks of the creek all afternoon. But as the day wore on, the hours brought him no closer to a decision.

When he passed the shallow singing rapids, the music he and Holly had heard at the swimming hole caught his ear. Around a curve in the creek, Holly's image smiled at him from a quiet pool, and when he broke the reflection with a stone, John Scott appeared in her place. Pausing at a tree which slanted out over the water, he remembered the cool touch of her hand on his brow at the giant sink.

Then, all at once, his decision was clear. Love had found a way. He turned back toward the camper.

The ordeal was his. Holly must not bear it. The greatest of the suffering must be his. He had given John Scott his word. There was no other way.

Luke slowly and methodically began to prepare his camper for travel.

Chapter Twelve

After supper that evening Luke appeared at the cabin. Holly was in the kitchen washing the dishes and, to her surprise, Luke, instead of stopping to talk to John Scott a few minutes, came into the kitchen, washed his hands, and picked up the dish towel. The situation was very much like that first night she had met Luke and for some vague reason it sent a little chill scurrying up her spine.

"Would you walk with me this evening?" Luke asked, breaking the silence that had been between them since their brief greeting.

"I'd like that, Luke," Holly glanced up at him as she straightened the little checkered cloth on the kitchen table. There was a strange distant expression in his eyes and a hardness about the set of his mouth.

As they walked out on the porch, the first shade of evening had settled a soft mantle on the hills, closing off the valley from the rest of the world. The early evening stars, luminous faraway worlds, were visible in the deep blue-gray sky.

"We're going for a walk, Daddy," Holly said, glancing at her father. There was something different about him, too, but she didn't know what it was. It tugged at her heart, and she impulsively leaned over and kissed his forehead.

"Tomorrow's a school day, Holly," he gruffly reminded her.

"I know, Daddy," she said, smiling at him before she and Luke walked down the steps of the cabin.

They strolled around the great circle, pausing half way across the wooden bridge that spanned Mill Creek. It was one of those rare days when the park was almost deserted. A few distant specks of light were the only witness to campers remaining in the park.

Why, she thought, *it's as if Luke and I are the only two people in the whole world at this moment.* And in a way she was right, for Tannehill was the only world she had ever known. Neither of them spoke, as they walked in the clear cool night air.

Downstream, the furnaces stood in majestic silence, lonely dark monoliths of the past, flanked by evergreens and distant folds of mountains. The water flowed gently down the placid stream and murmured over the shallow rapids, blending with the music of the pines, echoing the tale of the men who had toiled on the banks of Roupe's Creek, echoing a song of the past.

Then Holly knew—she knew that tomorrow Luke would be a part of her past and there would be another stanza in the song of Tannehill. She remembered the pledge she had made to herself at the church. She turned to Luke.

"You're leaving aren't you, Luke?"

"Yes. In the morning—early."

"Then this is our last walk together," she said, trying to phrase her words as if he were just another camper who had come to Tannehill. There was a false lightness to her voice. "I'll miss you."

"I'll miss this place...and I'll miss you Holly." Luke's words were grave, guarding his own secret.

"You've finished all your work?" she asked.

"Yes." It had been done long ago, he reflected, but he had just put off leaving, using his vacation to extend his stay.

"Well, then, I guess we'd better be getting back since you're going to start early. You'll want to get through Birmingham before the morning traffic."

They turned and walked back across the bridge toward the old store.

No clinging vine, my Holly, he thought. *She's strong enough to take whatever life deals her.*

"There's no sense in your walking way back up to the cabin, Luke. We'll just say good-bye here." *I've got to have some time alone before I go back to the cabin,* she thought desperately. *Daddy might still be awake and I can't face him—not yet.*

Luke looked at her curiously for a moment and then he understood. He needed some time himself.

"Perhaps you're right, Holly," he said.

"Good-bye, Luke," she tilted her chin up in that tiny familiar gesture of defiance.

That was his undoing. "Not yet, Holly," he pulled her into his arms.

Holly turned her head away and tried to push away from him.

"No, Luke, don't kiss me."

"Holly," he murmured against her hair.

"No!" she said fiercely. "I don't want your pity."

"Is that what you think I feel?" Luke's voice was almost harsh. The vivid blue of his eyes was reflected by the light of the moon just before a cloud darkened the bisque sphere.

As they moved into the shelter of the store's porch,

Holly faced the one thing she had stubbornly avoided—he was leaving and he had not so much as hinted at a word of love, or even affection.

"What else?" she asked as she continued outwardly to resist him, for her heart, coward that it was, would have welcomed his kiss.

Luke knew there was no answer he could give at this moment, for the truth would lead Holly into more pain and grief and perhaps a decision she would regret. So he said nothing. He drew her against him and set his mouth on hers.

Resistance went out of Holly as she surrendered to the glory of Luke's kiss. He shifted her slender form closer against him and threaded his fingers through her hair.

Holly tried to hold on to the thought that to Luke it was only a farewell embrace. But it was Luke who ended the kiss.

"Luke," she whispered, words tumbling out that she had vowed to keep locked inside, "I love you." Her voice faltered as she looked into eyes that were masked by darkness. Then she tore herself from his arms.

Luke let her go. He had longed to hear those words, and words would have to be enough. He watched her until she disappeared into the shadows of her cabin.

For a long time Luke stood on the porch of the old country store and looked out over the circle. He watched silver and black compositions appear upon the earth only to be erased by feathery clouds racing with the moon.

The morning sun slumbered behind the hills, casting an eerie deep pink glow in the sky above the timber. Luke checked the campsite one last time. He had already checked everything at least three times.

There's no use putting it off any longer, he thought. *I'm just trying to delay the inevitable—trying to put off leaving Holly.*

Luke looked for the last time on the artistry of the Tannehill daybreak, then climbed into the station wagon and slammed the door. He glanced at a dejected Brandy as he turned the key and slowly pulled out into the circle.

I'll drive past the Scott cabin once more, he thought. *I'll look one last time.* He turned the wrong way so he could drive past the first cabin on the way out. His headlights were the only lights in the park.

As he pulled in front of the cabin, the headlights cast a golden beam through the pines and captured Holly. She sat just as Luke had first seen her—on the front porch of that old log cabin, her arms about one knee, her chin tilted a bit defiantly. Buddy was asleep at her side.

There was nothing he could do except stop the car. Holly quickly ran across the small bridge to the car window.

"Good morning, Luke."

"Did you get any sleep?" he asked.

"No."

Luke looked at her eyes, violet shadows visible in the dawning light. He saw a faint redness around the rims.

"You've been crying."

"Yes, but I put lots of cold water on my face. I didn't want you to know."

"I don't mind your crying today, Holly. But no more. Don't you cry anymore—understand?" His voice was stern but there was a tiny twitch at the edge of his mouth, which betrayed his emotions, if Holly had but seen it.

"Yes, Luke," she said obediently. "But don't you worry about my crying. Daddy says it's good for the soul. He says men would be better off if they could cry. You know, 'Blessed are they that mourn for they shall be comforted.' I don't think that's exactly what it means, but I don't argue much with Daddy."

"Just what do you think it means?"

She looked into the depths of his eyes, remembering how she had felt that first night when she had thought the whole world might be reflected there. She had been right. She had dared to look and that's what she had found—her world.

"Why, it means that those who weep or mourn for others, not themselves, shall in the end be comforted."

"Holly, are you sure you're just twenty-one?" a smile played at the corners of his mouth.

She smiled back at him. "You sounded just like Daddy then." She lowered her voice and spoke in the soft Alabama drawl of her father, trying to make the conversation light and carefree.

"Take care, Holly." Luke turned the key in the ignition. His smile was gone.

"Luke, let me ride up to the end of the circle with you,…" she crushed a little sob that rose in her throat and tried to make her voice normal.

"That won't make it easier, Holly," he said, not fooled by her small act of bravery.

"I don't mind, Luke. Love's never easy, you know. The goods and bads are all mixed together." She held her breath until he answered.

"Get in," he spoke almost harshly as he reached over and opened the door for her. Holly ran around the front of the car and slipped into the seat. She reached back and stroked Brandy, then sat very still as Luke drove around the circle. Neither of them spoke.

When they reached the beginning of the main road, Luke stopped the car and cut off the headlights. Holly broke the silence.

"Luke, I want you to have this as a remembrance of Tannehill…and me." Holly pulled her little New Testament from her pocket. It was wrapped in the linen square she had embroidered that Sunday afternoon. She had completed the Tannehill pine, and now gracefully looped around the trunk was the letter L. She held it out to him.

Their fingers touched as he took the gift and then she was in his arms, her face pressed in the hollow of his shoulder, her slender arms about his neck, her small rounded figure pressed tightly against him.

I can't kiss her, he thought. *If I do, I won't have the strength to leave. If I do….* He dropped his arms and clenched his fists.

For a long moment she clung to him. Then she realized he was not returning her embrace. She slowly removed her arms and sat back in the seat.

"Seems I've been doing all the holding, Luke."

She reached for the handle and opened the door. Abruptly, she turned back to him.

"I just have to ask you, Luke. I wasn't going to. I told myself I wouldn't, but I have to." The words rushed out in a torrent, like water when a dam breaks. "Luke, you act like you care for me…sometimes…and you kissed me last night like you cared for me, but I've never been in love before. I've never even kissed a man like this before, so maybe I've read too much into things. Luke,…." she took a deep breath, "Luke, do you love me?"

He groaned as he reached for her and pulled her

across the car seat into his arms. He kissed her with all the passion he had hidden, with all the agony of parting, kissed her for all the lonely days that were ahead for him, kissed her as he had dreamed of doing since the first day he had seen her.

Holly didn't move. She was very still, acutely aware of the answer in his kiss. Her heart took wings. He loved her—this was real. Even if he never said it, she knew. The petal smoothness of her lips moved under his as she returned his kiss.

"Holly," he spoke her name like a tormented caress as he lifted his head from hers.

She heard the agony in his voice, and her heart stopped in flight. Like Icarus, she had soared too close to the sun and she would have to pay the price.

"There's someone between us, isn't there, Luke?" She dared not look into his eyes as she asked, so she concentrated on the pulse at the base of his throat.

"Yes, Holly."

"Someone...someone you've made a commitment to, Luke?"

"Yes." He pulled her head against his shoulder, his hand cradling her head.

"Someone you don't want to hurt?"

"Most of all, someone I don't want to hurt." The agony was back in his voice again, and it touched her heartstrings.

"Oh, Luke,..." she pulled away from him. "I didn't mean to say all those things, or cause you any pain. I know I have no claim on you. I know you have a different way of life—one that doesn't include me." Her face was stricken.

Luke still needed to say one more thing, so he steeled himself and said it. "Holly, listen to me carefully. This is your senior year in college, one of the

157

best years of your life. There'll be ball games and parties, and maybe someone else in your life very soon. You're only twenty-one and—"

She touched her small fingertips to his lips, stopping him in mid-sentence. "Don't say that. I can't bear it."

Neither can I, Holly, he thought. *Neither can I.* His arms went around her again, drawing her against him. He rested his face against her hair.

"Holly, were you listening?"

"Yes, Luke."

"I want this to be the best year of your life, Holly. I want you to make it that way for me. Will you try?"

"Yes, Luke," she promised, knowing that he had already made it the most wonderful year of her life, even if she never saw him again.

As tears fought their way into her eyes, she moved out of his arms. She couldn't cry now, not after she had held back this long. She wouldn't let him see her tears.

"Good-bye, Luke," she whispered just before she jumped out of the car and slammed the door. As she crossed the road and ran toward the cabin, the tears tumbled down her face. She ran across the bridge, past the cabin and up the path to the furnace trail, Buddy at her heels.

At the moment Holly and Buddy reached the top of the hill, the sun spilled over the trees and framed a young woman and her dog against the beauty of the Alabama morning.

"Holly, I love you. I love you more than life." Luke's voice was clear and vibrant in the car but only Brandy was there to hear.

Then Holly and Buddy were gone and all that was left was the glorious Tannehill sunrise and the melodious song of the morning.

Chapter Thirteen

It *was* one of the best years of Holly's life, because the love she had for Luke did not diminish. It burned as brightly through the dark wintry days as it had in the brilliant fall sunshine before he left. It was as sweet on the day the dogwoods bloomed as when the first snow had fallen. It was as pure and clear when the spring rains came as when the last autumn leaf had drifted to earth.

Luke's love for her, and her love for him, became a part of Holly's existence, and like true knowledge, it changed her life. She unconsciously became the person she thought would please him, not aware that for Luke, she did not need to change.

"You're different, Holly," Charles said for the second time that week.

"Different?" Holly stepped behind the counter at the store to keep him company since there were no customers waiting to be served. The early November rain had been steady for two days, and only four campers were left in the park. She watched Charles as he restocked the shelves. "How am I different?"

"I don't exactly know, but you are." He straightened up and studied her and as usual he could find no fault with anything he saw. "Maybe it's the way you talk or the way you dress."

Holly laughed as she glanced down at her faded jeans and checked shirt.

"Aw...Holly, I saw you last Sunday with your hair all piled on top of your head like a fashion model in the magazines." Charles turned back to his work.

"You can't very well wear jeans to church," Holly spoke with feigned indignity.

"You study more, too," said Charles lamely, realizing that he wasn't making his point very clearly.

"This is my last year of college. I've just been thinking I'd better make the most of it, Charlie." But down deep inside, Holly knew that wasn't the whole of it. She studied more because of Luke; she watched her grammar because of Luke; when she occasionally wore a sophisticated hairstyle, it was because of Luke. What she didn't realize was that her whole lifestyle was revolving around Luke and what might have been.

Charles wasn't the only one to notice the change in Holly. John Scott saw it, too. Holly, his little girl, was a woman now. She contained her sorrowful love eloquently, never complaining, never looking back, secure in the knowledge that Luke loved her and that he had made the right decision. For Holly, there was never any question of Luke's living a life without honor, and if the person between them was that important to Luke, then there could be no alternative. Holly's knowledge of his love for her was enough.

John Scott respected no man more than he did Luke Westford. John knew he was dying, and the prospect of facing his last days without Holly would have been unbearable. His Holly, who smiled so sweetly as she went about her work; his Holly, who sang softly as she sat on the porch with him in the evenings; his Holly, who would comfort him in his last days.

Holly tried—she really tried. She did all those things that are supposed to make the last year in college a memorable one. She did everything she had promised Luke she would do.

Not long after Luke left, she had two invitations to the homecoming football game. She accepted Charlie's, inwardly admitting she did so because she knew he would not compromise her, not even to the point of expecting an affectionate goodnight kiss.

Charlie kept up a steady stream of conversation and quips as they drove to the university that Saturday, and Holly contributed her share of the talk. Although her enthusiasm of past years was missing, she was determined to enjoy the occasion. So she smiled, and greeted old friends, and acted out her part.

The stadium was packed and Charles held her hand as they threaded through the crowds, up the steps and down a narrow aisle to their seats. There in the student section, amid her fellow classmates, the sorrow of Luke's leaving was suppressed. The color-splashed crowds made her feel less lonely, and her little red and white hat with its red grosgrain ribbon temporarily raised her sinking spirits.

She did have one terrible moment at half time as the university band marched through formations across the field and a giant letter L emerged—a graceful curve of dashing uniforms, decorated with golden horns and drums.

"Holly," Charlie's voice shattered the illusion, "here's your Coke."

"Thanks,..." she answered, relieved that the haunting L had melted into another formation.

When Charles reached across and took her hand, she didn't withdraw her fingers. She took refuge in his touch, unmindful that for Charles, there was more to it than that.

Winter brought with it routine. Charles picked Holly up in the mornings, they made the trip to the university, attended classes, and returned to Tannehill. In the afternoons, after Holly and Buddy went for a walk, she fixed supper and washed dishes. Frequently, Charles came to the cabin after he finished work at the store to study with Holly.

John Scott never voiced his thoughts when he saw their two heads close together over their notes or a thick history text. Nor did he comment when he heard their laughter as Charles coaxed her into forgetting the past, or when he noticed the longing in Charles's eyes in an unguarded moment. John Scott just sat by the fire, smoked his pipe, and silently remarked to himself that his daughter didn't need any more problems than the ones she already had.

Sundays were the best and the worst of times. Faithfully, Holly and John made their way up the hill to the church. Holly loved to sing the old hymns, especially the ones so many larger churches had abandoned and which were not included in the newer hymnals. The little church was suffused with songs of praise that drifted out across the hills toward the heavens.

But along with the songs came memories. More than once, Holly had to remind herself to keep her thoughts on the sermon.

Sunday afternoons, when campers customarily packed up their gear and drove away, brought a special sadness. The campers dwindled as the days grew colder and shorter, so Holly had fewer odd jobs around the park. Only on rare occasions were there enough visitors for Charles to need her at the camp store. So more than one Sunday afternoon Holly spent in the kitchen, her elbows propped on the table, read-ing from her Bible.

Charlie came for Christmas dinner bearing his ab-surd version of the twelve gifts of Christmas. He had tied twelve small boxes to a pine bough. One con-tained a new pipe for John Scott, one a silver bracelet for Holly, and the other ten were promises to take Holly to all *his* favorite films at the university's spring film series.

During the holidays, Charlie was at the cabin at every opportunity, and he produced tickets to the New Year's Eve triple movie extravaganza at the Alabama Theater in Birmingham. So Holly saw the old year out and the new in with Paul Newman, Robert Redford, and Dustin Hoffman—and Charlie. She reminded her-self to be fascinated by the Moorish motif and the hall of mirrors at the theater and remembered to laugh in all the right places. When the massive Wurlitzer pipe organ rose from beneath the floor and filled the the-ater with a symphonic blast, Holly resolutely joined Charlie and the other three thousand movie goers un-der the elliptical dome in singing "Auld Lang Syne."

The new year brought a big change in Holly's life. In January she began a semester of student teaching at a Tuscaloosa high school near the university. The de-manding schedule taxed her energy and she found less time to think of Luke. But even the classroom had its pitfalls—like ninth grade world geography when no matter what part of the world was being mapped, her eyes strayed to Iowa.

Spring flowers finally sprinkled the hills and the shadows of winter gathered in the forest for the flight north. But for Holly, who had once thrilled to every tiny new green bud, the days seemed all the same.

Spring brought still another change—a subtle difference in her relationship with Charlie. One evening in mid-April Holly and Charlie had driven to the campus to see one of the film series.

"Only one more present to go," Charlie said, as he cut the motor of the Mustang.

"Charlie, you're impossible," Holly laughed.

"Yes, I know," he agreed immodestly.

"I had a wonderful time," she concluded as he reluctantly walked her to the door of the cabin. It was true. She always enjoyed the film series and his company. "I'll see you tomorrow afternoon, Charlie."

"Wait, Holly." Charles closed the screen door she had half way opened. "I've got a surprise to tell you— something I've been saving for a special occasion. I guess this is special enough."

"Very special, Charlie," Holly agreed, smiling at the little-boy eagerness on his face. "Besides, I can see you're dying to tell me."

"I've been accepted at law school next fall."

"Oh, Charlie, that's marvelous!" Impulsively, Holly leaned forward and kissed his cheek. And before she quite knew what was happening, he had kissed her on the mouth. It was a friendly kiss, and in view of the circumstances, she did not protest.

"You're going to know a real live lawyer," Charlie said hurriedly, almost as if he dared not give her time to reconsider what had passed between them. "That just might come in handy."

For once Charlie couldn't think of a clever exit line. He turned, backed up a few paces, clicked his heels and ended the evening with an extravagant bow.

The spring turned into a brilliant summer, the diamond constellations of the season dotting the sky.

Finally even the austere memory of winter faded in the Alabama heat.

Summer passed faster than Holly had ever thought possible. There was a flurry of studying for exams in July and August and then graduation.

The morning of graduation Larry Jacobs's delivery truck bumped to a stop in front of the cabin. Holly was in the bathroom carefully applying a coat of coral lipstick that exactly matched her sleeveless, shirred shell and softly flared skirt. It was a hot, stifling day and Holly dreaded the long ceremony ahead. She forced herself to think about the friendly hospitality of Charlie's mother who had invited her and her father to a celebration buffet at the Bradley home.

It's time I thought about the future, she insisted to herself, *not the past.*

At the sound of the truck door, Holly replaced the lipstick in its case and went to the front porch. Larry swung open the back door of the truck and lifted a magnificent vase of red roses from the box where it had been wedged for safety. He held it aloft like a trophy as he came across the bridge and up the steps.

"Who's Luke?" he asked, and without waiting for her to answer he rattled on, "You sure must have made some impression on him."

"And how do you know who they're from?" Holly questioned, trying to hide the terrible wave of weakness that flooded through her.

"Curiosity got the best of me, Holly," Larry admitted with chagrin, "besides, we don't deliver flowers like this every day. It cost a fortune. Just look at that vase."

The arrangement was a work of art. The beautiful cut glass vase was tall and bell shaped at the bottom with the neck flared at precisely the right angle. A dozen elegant crimson roses stood regally poised on

165

long stems, luminous and fragrant, defiantly resisting the August heat. Holly couldn't suppress a little gasp of pleasure at the sight of the flowers.

"You'd make a great postman, Larry," Holly laughed good-naturedly. "Think of all the fun you could have reading people's post cards."

"I'm not as nosy as you think, Holly. We've been so busy, I've had to help out in the shop. I stuffed the envelopes."

"Now when they let you work in the back with all those beautiful vases—that's busy," Holly declared.

"I'll put this inside for you," Larry offered. "It's kinda heavy."

Holly opened the door and cleared off one of the end tables for the bouquet. Even before Larry placed the roses on the table, the room seemed filled with Luke's presence.

"Well, who is he?" Larry asked again. "Was he that guy I saw you with at the church last fall?"

"Would you like a Coke?" Wild horses couldn't have pulled any information about Luke out of her at that moment.

"I can take a hint." Larry moved toward the door. "Besides, I got lots of cards to read before I finish for the day."

Holly followed him out to the steps. As he stepped up into the truck, he called a farewell.

"I almost forgot. Congratulations, Teach."

Holly went back into the quiet of the cabin and pulled the little card from the envelope. It read, "Luke"—no more, no less. Though she read it a dozen times, once for each rose, she couldn't make it say any more.

Just before it was time for her father to come in from his morning rounds and dress for the exercises, Holly pulled the card from the envelope for the last time and placed it between the pages of her Bible.

At last Holly had that certificate. She was a teacher. She refused to admit to herself that she lacked the enthusiasm for it that she once had. And, as it turned out, the only available position for a history teacher in the county that fall was miles away.

The summer crowds at Tannehill continued to be unusually large and the traffic unusually hectic. When Charles gave up his afternoon job to enter law school, Holly consented to work one more semester in the camp store and help her father.

However, something more important influenced her final decision. There was a stoop to John Scott's shoulders that hadn't been there before. A tired gray line gathered about his mouth by supper time each day, and he seemed to spend more and more time in his rocking chair.

Yes, thought Holly, *there will be time enough to teach next semester. Perhaps in January, there will be an opening close to home.*

The days passed slowly and uneventfully, the hot oppressing summer finally cooled by fall. In late October, Indian summer flooded the valley with radiant splendor.

It was on a beautiful cloudless day in the last week of October that John Scott sat down in his rocking chair and went to sleep for the last time. He had placed his rocker to catch the last rays of the afternoon sun to warm his bones, which seemed chilled even on such a warm day. That Tuesday the park was strangely empty for such beautiful weather. The weekend crowd had departed, and only a few new campers had arrived.

The woods were peaceful and serene. The sun angled through the trees and touched the cabin, casting a golden glow across the circle in front of the house, highlighting a bird returning to its nest, and sprinkling gold dust on a chipmunk that scurried behind a rock.

Through the golden mist John Scott saw the past then the future. He saw Holly and Luke, and then as the veil lifted and those golden images receded, he saw clearly the beloved face of Rebecca. The tired look he had worn for so long was replaced by a faint smile as his pipe slipped from his grasp and fell to rest on the worn planks of the front porch.

When Holly and Buddy returned from their evening run through the woods after closing the store, the sun had fallen behind the mountains and the shadows had flung a cloak of grey over the park.

How peaceful Daddy looks, thought Holly as she and Buddy bounded up the steps of the cabin. Then she saw his pipe and the ashes scattered on the rough planks and the stilled rim of the rocker.

John Scott had heard an eternal song, a heavenly strain beckoning through earth's gathering shadows. There on the porch of their old log cabin, he quietly and joyfully gave himself to his Lord amid the immortal melody of peace.

Chapter Fourteen

The memory of the peace on John Scott's face, the knowledge of Luke's love and Charles's company sustained Holly through the days that followed the funeral. She didn't remember a lot about the simple service at the little Tannehill church because all the memories of her father filled up her mind and because that was what she wanted to remember.

But there were some things Holly would never forget. Charlie's parents had offered their assistance in making the funeral arrangements. Rangers and workers filled the little cabin, sat on the porch, and talked of John Scott. Scores of people Holly didn't know came to offer condolences. Time after time they introduced themselves with the same quiet phrase.

"Miss Scott, I know you don't know me but...."

The ladies of the church stocked the kitchen with food and coffee, washed stacks of dishes and tidied up the cabin.

Miss Beulah Scott, Holly's aunt and her only relative, came up from Mobile. Miss Beulah, fifteen years older than John, had raised him after their parent's death. She had never married. Several years had slipped by since their last visit together, so Holly and

Aunt Beulah talked long into the night after the funeral. And after Miss Beulah left, Holly found an envelope of old family pictures of her father tucked under one of the Dutch Girl pillows.

Even though Holly had requested that instead of flowers, contributions be made to the Alabama Nongame Wildlife Fund, flowers overflowed the cabin and the country church.

The crowd overflowed the church, too, and people stood outside during the service. But the comforting words of the minister and the heartfelt hymns wafted out the open windows and made everyone feel included. Then they all stood together in the old cemetery and said their last good-byes to John Scott.

The afternoon after Aunt Beulah left, Charlie came to the cabin. He tried to coax Holly to ride into Bessemer for a hamburger, thinking it would do her good to get away for a while, but they ended up making sandwiches from the leftovers stuffed in the refrigerator.

Charlie stayed long after his usual leaving time, reluctant to leave Holly alone in the cabin. However, the time finally came when Holly and Buddy had to close the door and admit the reality of being alone. Her father was gone.

John Scott was gone.

"You'll like serving on the moot jury, Holly," Charles insisted as they drove up the university driveway. "Moot court is one of the most interesting things about law school."

It had almost taken an act of Congress to persuade Holly to serve as a juror. Charles thought of it as his toughest case. The only thing he took as seriously as his law studies was making certain that he was there when Holly needed him. More and more since her father's death she had refused his invitations. So they had spent a lot of hours just sitting in the porch swing, or when it was too cold, listening to music in the living room of the cabin. But in this instance, Charles won his case.

"It does sound interesting, Charlie," Holly agreed. "It would even sound better if you were the defending or prosecuting attorney."

"My turn will come, probably before I'm ready for it."

"You're right about that. Lots of things seem to happen before we're ready for them."

"Maybe it's not such a good idea for you to serve on the jury after all, Holly. I don't see how people are going to keep their minds on what they're doing when they see you in that dress." Charles determinedly chased the little shadow of the past away.

Her blue chambray dress with its white eyelet-lace inset from shoulder to waist, button-band collar and cuffs, suited Holly perfectly. The smooth line of her hair and small pearl earrings completed the simple but striking effect.

"I think they've been teaching you something over here besides law," Holly responded to his compliment.

"There's more than one way to win a case," Charles announced with fake hauteur.

"It boggles my mind to think of you turned loose in a courtroom, Charlie. How can you lose with John Wayne, Jimmy Stewart, and heaven knows who else in your repertoire."

Charles pulled the car into a parking place, cut the ignition, and went around to help Holly from the car.

"Who would you like for me to be today?" he asked, taking her hand as they walked past the chapel toward the law school building.

171

"We'd better hurry," Holly answered, but the clock atop the library building showed there was plenty of time.

Another little memory wafted across their path, but Charlie just seized the opportunity to build up Holly's low spirits.

"Yes," he said, walking faster, "I want to show you off. Everybody thinks I've made you up from my over-active imagination."

Charles escorted her into the foyer of the Law School, and Holly was struck by a sense of awe. From the huge chandelier to the gold velvet seat pads, the school cast an aura of heritage and drama. The moot courtroom, Holly decided, was more impressive than the real thing. No wonder that the walls were lined with the portraits of famous graduates.

Holly smiled to herself. They really did teach something besides law—a desire to serve and achieve was that extra item that went along with a respected diploma.

As it turned out, Charlie didn't need to do much showing off, for Holly made her own impact. A lot of heads turned in her direction and lingered on the slim figure that brought an aura of freshness and beauty into the room.

During the course of the trial, the defense attorney walked to the jury box and looked straight into her eyes as he questioned a witness and won his case with a few well-chosen words.

After court was adjourned, he demanded an introduction, and Holly learned that he was a friend of Charles. Marc McCain, as forceful off center-stage as on, insisted that Holly and Charles join a group of law students for a celebration party. To Holly's relief, Charles declined for them. On the way to the car,

Charles mentioned the party.

"I didn't think you'd want to go, Holly."

"No, Charlie, I didn't. I'd just rather be with you." If she had looked at him, Holly might have seen how much her words pleased him.

They drove up the mountain to a little restaurant on the highway. Charles talked about the good points of the defense in the court case and told anecdotes about his favorite professor. Four hamburgers and two Cokes later, they sat companionably in the booth listening to the clatter of sound in the crowded restaurant.

"You know something, Charlie?" Holly asked. "Remember last year when you said I was different? Well, you're different now."

"Am I, Holly?"

"You look like a Philadelphia lawyer with that distinguished three-piece, gray suit and white shirt, and your curls all smoothed out."

"Do you realize what I have to go through to get this effect?" he groaned. "Sometimes I have a sort of nightmare. I'm up giving the defense summation in the most important court case of the year, and my hair forgets. Curl by curl it pops up. The jury just sits there and stares at my hair."

Holly laughed. "Remember that time we waded in Mill Creek and you fell in and you combed your hair a dozen times on the way home so your mom wouldn't know?"

"It was all your fault. Or do you remember that part? You just had to have that rock on the bottom."

"It's been a long time since we waded in Mill Creek."

"Then let's go wade in it again. Right now," he demanded.

"Charlie, you're crazy." Holly laughed again. "What would I do without you?"

"Nothing I hope," he quipped, but beneath those flippant words there burned a steadfast hope.

But Charlie's company wasn't enough to uphold her through the trouble that descended the second week of November when a letter arrived from the Tannehill Furnace and Foundry Commission. There was to be a new park superintendent. Of course she had known that all along, but to have it in writing was different; it was like an ultimatum that signaled an end to her life at Tannehill. That thought had never been real to her before. It had always been far off in the future and she had never really faced it. Now the loss of the only home she had ever really known was thrust upon her along with the loss of her father.

And Buddy! Where would they live and what would they do without her father and Tannehill? She had never even had a job before except for her work at the store, and though the insurance money would last a little while, it would be gone all too soon.

She read and reread the letter. The new superintendent would arrive at the first of December. There would be a new residence constructed for him and his family, but until it was completed, they would occupy the old cabin.

That night she sat on the front porch and slipped her arms about Buddy's neck and shed the first tears since her father's death.

"Oh, Buddy," she buried her face in the soft fur on the top of the dog's head, "I can't bear to think of you leaving Tannehill and being penned up in a little yard somewhere. And when I get a job, I'll be gone all day."

Buddy looked at her with solemn eyes, then laid his head in her lap as if to assure her that as long as they

174

were together, everything would turn out just fine.

"You're right, Buddy," she whispered, "we'll just have to face tomorrow together. Tomorrow we'll look for a place to move."

But when tomorrow came, things were worse, because all the places advertised in the paper were either too expensive, or had no yard, or didn't allow pets.

As it eventually turned out, the only place she could afford with a fenced yard was a wretched little apartment in the basement of an old rambling house in Bessemer. She knew her heart would ache when she went to work each day and left Buddy in that lonely place. Buddy, who had roamed the woods all his life, wouldn't understand such confinement, but she agreed to send the deposit and to move at the end of November.

That evening after law school, Charles drove over to see Holly.

"How'd it go, Holly?" He lowered himself into the couch beside her.

"I found a place," she said, but her eyes revealed to him just how awful it was.

"Holly, I talked to the Harpers today. They can put you up in their back room. It isn't big, but I could help you fix it up."

She smiled at that, thinking of the Harpers' modest little home and how, when their daughter and her family came to visit, they had to make pallets on the floor for the children.

"That's very kind of them, Charlie, but I couldn't do that. It wouldn't be fair to them. Besides, I've got to get a job. Daddy's insurance money won't last forever." Her chin trembled a little, then she lifted it courageously.

"Would you like for me to watch after Buddy? We

could sort of share him and you could come out here every weekend."

"Oh, Charlie, I can't lose Buddy, too." Her voice quivered just thinking about going back to that dark little basement every evening without Buddy there to greet her. No, whatever happened, they would just have to tough it out together.

"Well, then," Charles burst out, "you'll just have to marry me, Holly. You can't go and live in Bessemer all by yourself. Why you never even worked before and everybody knows cities aren't safe after dark anymore. Why some of them aren't safe in daylight!"

Holly stared at Charles. All this time she had been so busy feeling sorry for herself, she hadn't thought about Charles. She had been so blind, she hadn't seen that he loved her. She reached out and laid her hand on his arm for a moment and looked into that beloved boyish face. She was touched by his offer and the pleading in his voice.

"Charlie, I'm sorry. I never meant for you to feel that way about me. I care for you, but not like that."

Charles looked down at his fingers and switched his car keys from one hand to the other.

"I know you love Luke, Holly, but he's not coming back. Your daddy told me he hasn't even kept in touch. He could have written you." Charles shuffled his feet against the rug. "Maybe you could learn to love me, Holly."

"No, Charlie," she said quietly.

He continued to speak as if he hadn't heard her. "I could borrow some money from the bank and we could buy a trailer and find a place near here. They might even let us use one of the campsites permanently. You'll get a teaching position in January. Holly, we can make it together."

"Charlie, listen to me," she pleaded. "I don't love you that way. I love you like a brother."

The light went out of his eyes then, and Holly knew he had finally heard her message. But in those brief moments while Charles had tried to persuade her, Holly had thought of living in the confined area of a trailer with Charles and of trying to fulfill the role of a wife. She had no other choice but to refuse.

Charles rose from the couch and went to the door.

"Holly, I'll always be here if you need me," Charles spoke from the shadow of the porch but Holly could see he wasn't looking at her. His head was bowed.

Holly ran to him and threw her arms about his neck.

"Oh, Charlie, I'll always love you in such a special way." She fought back the tears that threatened to fall.

"Hey,..." he muttered gently, enfolding her into his arms and pressing a little kiss to her hair, "you're ruining my dramatic exit. I'm the star—remember?"

"Yes, Charlie, I'll always remember."

He put her gently from him, curled his mouth and pulled Bogey from his repertoire.

"Here's looking at you, kid."

The call of the wild turkeys heralded the coming of Thanksgiving. Thanksgiving without her father, without Luke, without her beloved Tannehill, was only a week away.

We'll go to our apartment, thought Holly, *and spend some time there. Perhaps we can get used to it before we have to move.* But even as she considered that action, she knew it wouldn't work.

The place was even worse than she had anticipated. After Buddy inspected the two little dark basement rooms and made three trips around the small fenced-in yard, he lay down with his head between his front paws. He was ready to go home.

"Now, Buddy," Holly said, looking around at the bare walls, "it isn't as bad as all that. I've thought of a great idea. I'm going to get placed on the supply teacher list. I'll be home every day at four. It won't even be dark. We can go for a run in the park and…" Her voice dropped at the expression in Buddy's eyes. He didn't believe a word of it—neither did she.

The Tuesday afternoon before Thanksgiving Holly and Charlie drove into Bessemer because he insisted on checking out the apartment she had rented. Charlie didn't say any of the things he wanted to say as he looked around the small dismal rooms Holly was forced to trade for her cabin, but his lack of humor revealed his feelings. They drove back to the highway in silence.

"I'll help you move, Holly," Charlie finally offered. "We can use Dad's pickup. It'll cut down a lot on your expenses, and I know he'll help." He unconsciously sailed through a caution light and merged with the traffic.

"Thank you, Charlie." Holly flashed him a smile she didn't feel. She hesitated a moment, then said, "Would you help me with a few things Thursday?"

"Thursday? That's Thanksgiving, Holly. I was hoping you'd eat dinner with us and we could spend the day together. You don't have to move until the end of the month."

"This is the last weekend of the month," she reminded him. "I'd like to move my bed and some dishes Thursday so Buddy and I can spend the night in Bessemer."

"Holly,…" Charlie started to protest as he unconventionally switched lanes.

"And since you're out of school for the holidays, we

could move some more things Friday, and your Dad could help with the big pieces this weekend." Holly paused and waited for Charlie to object, but he didn't. He just stared at the road ahead.

"It would be better if Buddy got used to our new place before Monday, Charlie. I'm going to look for a temporary job until I can get on the supply teacher list."

Charlie didn't answer that either, because he didn't know how.

When they pulled up in front of the cabin, Charlie turned to Holly and caught her hand in his.

"Holly, are you sure you won't reconsider about Thanksgiving dinner? You can bring Buddy." That was his final argument.

Holly laughed as she withdrew her hand. "You're very persuasive, Perry Mason, but I'll see you after dinner Thursday."

Holly went into the cabin and pulled the boxes she had stacked in the closet into the middle of the room. She worked far into the night at the anguishing task of packing, for each item she folded, or wrapped, or stacked evoked a precious memory.

Wednesday, when it could be put off no longer, Holly tackled the job she had been dreading the most. She pulled her father's belongings from the closet and bureau drawers and began to sort them out. The items that might be used by some of the park workers or rangers were folded neatly into one stack, the things for the city's rescue mission into another.

Perhaps Charlie would like to keep this, she thought, as she placed the pipe Charles had given her father at Christmas back into its box.

John Scott's favorite pipe, the one that he always smoked on the porch, went into the box with her treasured mementos and the pictures of her parents from the etagere.

Holly was struck with the realization of how few worldly possessions her father had collected. John Scott had been an unusual man, demanding nothing from life, giving everything. The small cabin had been plenty large for his simple, nonacquisitive tastes.

After the last dish was wrapped in newspaper and safely tucked into a box, Holly slipped on a jacket and called to Buddy, who was dozing by the fireplace. As she opened the cabin door, she said aloud what she had been thinking all day.

"We've put it off long enough." She lifted her chin. "We're moving tomorrow. It's Thanksgiving, so we'll just be thankful that we have a place to move." Buddy trotted out the door behind her.

As they walked up the trail toward the furnace, Holly thought of her first Thanksgiving at Tannehill and others before that. Willie and Madge Harper, friends of Rebecca and John from the old days, always invited John and Holly for Thanksgiving dinner. But when Holly was old enough to realize that it brought such a painful sense of loss for her father, she insisted on preparing Thanksgiving dinner at home. She would never forget that first disaster she cooked and how her father gallantly ate every bite.

Then another scene unfolded—an Iowa farmhouse filled with laughter, a Thanksgiving table piled high with food, Luke at one end of the table and her at the other.

Unconsciously Holly turned her steps toward the church. As she and Buddy walked the familiar path through the pines, she became aware of the stillness in the early darkness. There was not so much as a breath of song on the wind or a whisper of music in the leaves. It was if the whole world was hushed before Him, awaiting the dawning of Thanksgiving.

Holly repressed the persistent memories, bidding her soul, as well, to be silent before the Lord.

The moon slipped above the hills, shedding its light on the silent waiting world, antiquing the pine boughs and staining the church windows moon-white. Holly slipped through the door into a silvered sanctuary. The two pianos were flecked with moon dust.

She followed the moon-lit path to the altar and sank to her knees.

"Heavenly Father," she prayed, "I know you love me. You sacrificed your son that I might have life. I believe that your grace is sufficient for any hour, especially this one. I just want to thank you for the wonderful years I've spent at Tannehill with Daddy and for the days I had with Luke."

Buddy pushed the door of the church open and padded down the aisle. He nuzzled her hand.

"And thank you for Buddy," she added, smiling as she put her arms about his shaggy coat.

And there in the resplendent silver-coated world of the moon, Holly found solace and strength in His word that she had discovered in her heart:

"Casting all your care upon him; for he careth for you."

Chapter Fifteen

Thanksgiving Day spilled softly over the mountains into the valley. A single note of light followed by a brilliant crescendo of sunlight crested the trees and awakened the valley to a hymn of Thanksgiving.

At first glance it all looked the same to Luke Westford as he rounded the bend that afternoon. The hills were dappled with yellow and orange. In the distance the folds of mountains echoed with silver blues, misty grays, and soft greens. The cabins still flanked the circle, their roughhewn toughness giving evidence that they would be there for years to come.

Then Luke noticed the Furnace Master's Inn. It had been erected just across Mill Creek exactly as Holly had described it a year ago when they had visited the building site. The wide porch of the huge log cabin was an inviting place for guests to rest after an excellent meal. The second floor had five pairs of windows neatly curtained with ruffled tiebacks. A wide plank walk was constructed over the creek for easy access to the restaurant.

Still, there was a more important difference. As the blue Catalina moved around the Tannehill circle, Luke didn't see Holly sitting on the porch of the cabin. John

Scott's empty rocker was there, the swing swayed in lonely rhythm in the afternoon breeze, and marigolds nodded a greeting from the back yard. But Holly wasn't there.

As Luke pulled up behind a pickup truck parked in front of the cabin, Charlie walked out the door with a big box in his arms.

"Jumpin' Jehoshaphat!" Charlie almost dropped the dishes as he recognized the car. He stopped in his tracks and put the box down on the porch.

Buddy bounded from the trail behind the cabin just as Luke opened the car door. On the front seat, Brandy whined and trembled with anticipation and, after permission from Luke, ran to Buddy. The two dogs returned to Luke, Buddy's tail wagging furiously from side to side. Luke reached down to give Buddy a few vigorous pats before the dogs disappeared in the direction of the furnace.

Before Luke could cross the bridge, Charlie was there, pumping his hand. As they exchanged greetings, Luke's eyes went past Charlie to the door of the cabin.

"Holly's not here," Charlie said, inwardly acknowledging his surprise at being glad to see Luke Westford. "She's up at the church."

"Thanks, Charlie," Luke said, turning towards the trail. "And thanks for the letter."

"Quivering kumquats!" Charlie laughed as he sat down on the steps of the cabin. "W. C., I think Luke's got some 'definite pear-shaped ideas' to discuss with Holly!"

Luke found Holly in the old cemetery by the little Tannehill church. She wore faded jeans, a blue long-sleeved pullover shirt and old sneakers. A profusion of corn silk curls, longer than when he had last seen her, curtained her face. She was on her knees, packing the dirt around a newly planted rosebush, a hybrid that, in season, produced golden buds tipped with cerise, opening into yellow flowers edged in pink. The long stemmed, fragrant blossoms had been John Scott's favorite.

"Luke,..." Holly's voice trailed away after his name escaped her lips. She just stared at him, not quite able to believe he was real, afraid that if she so much as blinked her eyes, he would disappear.

But he was real. It was Luke. It was the Luke she had seen that first day, wearing an elegant dark blue suit and white shirt, except this time his shirt was unbuttoned at the throat.

He walked on up the hill and stopped beside the mound of earth where John Scott rested. He looked down at the small marker and a bouquet of bronze chrysanthemums that stood in a small vase in the Alabama clay.

"Your father was a fine man, Holly." Luke looked at Holly still kneeling beside the rose bush, small and slender, her hands covered with red mud. She was as strong and lovely as the bronze beauties that gracefully swayed in the afternoon sunlight.

Holly looked into Luke's eyes, into the blue ocean depths that had so haunted her dreams, and there was no more room for sorrow, only joy that he was here.

"It's the Peace rose," she said softly. "It was Daddy's favorite."

She ached to be in Luke's arms, to know the comfort of those strong shoulders, to feel the security of his embrace. But she couldn't go to him not knowing—not knowing if that someone was still between them.

"It's very beautiful," he said quietly. "I'm sure John Scott would be pleased."

"It may not live, being transplanted so late, but there's a chance." She sat back on her heels and pushed a wayward strand of hair away from her face with the back of a hand that trembled. Her legs felt strangely weak.

"There's every chance in the world, Holly." Luke came closer to where she was, restraining himself from gathering her into his arms and covering her face with kisses.

"You've come a long way to pay your respects, Luke. Daddy...and I thank you." She looked up at him. He seemed taller than she remembered, more handsome, stronger. She looked at the rosebush so that he could not see her eyes and read what was written in them. Her fingers absently touched the glossy leaves.

"How did you know about Daddy, Luke?"

"Charlie wrote to me. I didn't know until yesterday. I had been in Ohio for three weeks. The letter was waiting for me when I returned." Luke watched the small muddy fingers gently rubbing a speck of mud from a rose leaf.

"I know how busy your life is, Luke...."

"I didn't come just to pay my respects, Holly," he interrupted her, "I've come to take you home—if you still love me."

She sat very still, afraid to move, afraid she hadn't heard right. Then she lifted her face and looked into Luke Westford's eyes.

"If...if I still love you..." the words faded on her breath as she saw the unmasked love and passion in his face.

Holly sprang up from the ground and flung herself into Luke's arms. His arms held her close, his mouth touching her hair, her eyes, her lips.

She wound her arms about his neck, returning his kisses, whispering his name over and over.

"I love you, Holly." Luke made a trail of kisses across her face. "I've loved you since that first day I came to Tannehill and saw you on the porch."

After a few minutes, Holly drew away from Luke so she could look up at him. Her arms slipped from his neck so that her hands rested against his chest. Then she moved out of the circle of his arms and looked down at her father's grave. She turned her eyes to the mountains, smoky gray peaks vaulted by light drifting clouds.

"Luke, it was Daddy who stood between us, wasn't it?"

"Yes, Holly, it was."

"You knew he was dying, didn't you?"

"I found out the day before I left. You seemed so young, Holly, so innocent, still in college. At first I thought loving you was just a sort of madness on my part that would go away. But it didn't—it only got worse. I intended to talk to your father that Sunday but it just didn't work out the way I planned. That's when I came to the church."

"I remember, Luke." Holly looked out at the pine spires rising from the dwindling leaves of the hardwoods.

"After that Wednesday night when you came to my camper, I knew I couldn't wait any longer. So Thursday morning, I went back to see John. I intended to ask him if, after graduation you still felt the same about me, I could come for you. While we were talking, your father had an angina attack, Holly. We never finished that conversation."

"And that's when you decided to leave?"

"Yes."

"He asked you not to tell me, and I couldn't see his true condition because I couldn't bear to see it."

Holly turned and looked at Luke. He nodded his head in affirmation.

"Thank you, Luke, for loving me that much, for not making me face the choice I might have had to make. It's all so clear to me now, why you left the way you did, why you never said you loved me." Holly's voice was calm but the glitter of unshed tears touched the end of her lashes.

Luke closed the distance between them and drew her into the curve of his shoulder, laying his face against her hair.

"It's over now, Holly."

As Holly rested her head against his heart, she saw the edge of a linen handkerchief tipped with the green of Alabama pines in Luke's shirt pocket. The little New Testament was tucked inside. The pages were frayed; Luke had done a lot of reading.

"Holly, I know it hasn't been long enough since your father's death, but when you're feeling up to it we'll think about a wedding date."

"The Scotts never were much for putting off things, Luke." Holly lifted her head from the music of his heart and looked up at him.

With a low exclamation, he bent his head and kissed her.

"I don't think Daddy would have wanted us to wait, Luke." Holly spoke between kisses.

"I'm certain he wouldn't, Holly. Charlie wasn't the only one to write me. There was a letter from your father waiting for me when I got back, too. He asked me to come for you as soon as I could. He wanted to see us married before...." Luke held her close again, letting the words go unspoken.

Holly, in the security of Luke's embrace, heard a faint echoing through the hills, a woodland song she had never heard before.

"This is a fine place for a wedding, Holly, or we could be married at home."

"At home, Luke. Our home."

"We'll come back to Tannehill," Luke said, thinking of John Scott, knowing how Holly loved her father. He touched a kiss to her hair.

"We don't need to come back, Luke. My home is with you now. That little rosebush I planted was my way of saying good-bye to Tannehill." She looked up at him, her eyes clear and steady in the afternoon sunlight.

"Would you like to be alone here for a while, Holly? I can wait at the foot of the hill."

"Oh, no, Luke. I'll never be—or feel—alone again." She slipped her hand into his and he entwined their fingers.

Luke and Holly walked hand-in-hand down the little path from the old Tannehill cemetery. The woods were filled with bird songs and the music of nightingales.

Buddy and Brandy bounded from a side path and led the way down the winding trail. Luke and Holly paused at an opening in the trees to look out at Shades Mountain in the distance. The trees had turned to gold and silver and the hills to emerald and sapphire.

"We'll take what we can in the station wagon, Holly. Buddy and Brandy might be a little crowded, but we'll stop along the way. We'll ask Charlie to send the rest." Luke tightened his fingers about hers.

"It will take me a while to get ready," Holly cautioned, "at least ten minutes." She smiled at Luke— they laughed together.

Luke glanced down at his watch, then looked at Holly.

"We'll be home at sunrise tomorrow."

They began the descent down the hill and their steps quickened until they were running.

The wind stirred through the trees. The echo Holly had heard in the distance swelled and became a symphonic hymn, filling the church, the valley, and the hills with the breath of music.

This time Holly caught the melody. It was her father's favorite hymn. She heard her father's voice, deep joyful singing borne on the wind, mingled with the matchless song of Tannehill:

> "Sunrise tomorrow,
> sunrise tomorrow,
> Sunrise with Jesus
> for eternity."

Other Thomas Nelson Romances you will enjoy

Marylin Young

THE HEART OF THE STORM [No. 5]

Galveston legal secretary Melanie Hart and her employer Bret Stone, the man she loves, fight to save her ancestral home from land developers—and themselves from a deadly hurricane.

ISBN 0-8407-7354-4, $2.25

Jane Peart

LOVE TAKES FLIGHT [No. 4]

Trying to deny her love for playboy pilot T. J. Lang, Roblynn Mallory is forced to reevaluate her feelings when he is caught in a dangerous mid-air hijacking.

ISBN 0-8407-7353-6, $2.25

Irene Brand

A CHANGE OF HEART [No. 3]

Against her better judgment, teller Ginger Wilson is attracted to bank-owner Darren Banning, but she realizes a future with him is hopeless unless she unlocks the astonishing secret from his past.

ISBN 0-8407-7352-8, $2.25

Anna Lloyd Staton

THE CHALLENGED HEART [No. 2]

New York-based editor of a successful magazine, Cassandra Delaney falls for her wealthy boss—until she visits Kentucky horse country and meets a dedicated country doctor who challenges her big-city values.

ISBN 0-8407-7361-7, $2.25

Patricia Dunaway

IRISH LACE [No. 1]

When Texas-born Brenna Ryan embarks on a vacation to Ireland, the last thing she expects to do is fall in love with brooding Dr. Michael Larkin and attempt to change his attitude toward women.

ISBN 0-8407-7350-1, $2.25

Dear Reader:

I am committed to bringing you the kind of romantic novels you want to read. Please fill out the brief questionnaire below so we will know what you like most in romance.

Mail to: Etta Wilson
Thomas Nelson Publishers
P.O. Box 141000
Nashville, Tenn. 37214

1. Why did you buy this inspirational romance?

☐ Author
☐ Back cover description
☐ Christian story
☐ Cover art

☐ Recommendation from others
☐ Title
☐ Other_____

2. What did you like best about this book?

☐ Heroine
☐ Hero
☐ Christian elements

☐ Setting
☐ Story Line
☐ Secondary characters

3. Where did you buy this book?

☐ Christian bookstore
☐ Supermarket
☐ Drugstore

☐ General bookstore
☐ Book Club
☐ Other (specify)_____

4. Are you interested in buying other romances in this series?

☐ Very interested ☐ Somewhat interested
☐ Not interested

5. Please indicate your age group.
☐ Under 18 ☐ 25-34
☐ 18-24 ☐ 35-49 ☐ Over 50

6. Comments or suggestions?

7. Would you like to receive a free copy of the our romance newsletter? If so, please fill in your name and address.

Name _____

Address _____

City _____ State _____ Zip _____

7356-0